Educating

OPPOSITIONAL

AND DEFIANT

CHILDREN

Philip S. Hall • Nancy D. Hall

Association for Supervision and Curriculum Development
Alexandria, Virginia USA

Association for Supervision and Curriculum Development
1703 N. Beauregard St. • Alexandria, VA 22311-1714 USA
Telephone: 800-933-2723 or 703-578-9600 • Fax: 703-575-5400
Web site: http://www.ascd.org • E-mail: member@ascd.org

Gene R. Carter, *Executive Director*; Nancy Modrak, *Director of Publishing*; Julie Houtz, *Director of Book Editing & Production*; Tim Sniffin, *Project Manager*; Reece Quiñones, *Senior Graphic Designer*; Cynthia Stock, *Typesetter*; Vivian Coss, *Production Coordinator*

Printed in the United States of America.

s4/2003

ISBN: 0-87120-761-3   ASCD product no.: 103053
ASCD member price: $21.95   nonmember price: $25.95

Library of Congress Cataloging-in-Publication Data
Hall, Philip S., 1943–
    Educating oppositional and defiant children / Philip S. Hall, Nancy D. Hall.
        p.   cm.
"ASCD product no.: 103053"—T.p. verso.
Includes bibliographical references and index.
    ISBN 0-87120-761-3 (alk. paper)
    1. Problem children—Education—United States. 2. Classroom management—United States. I. Hall, Nancy D., 1951– II. Title.
LC4802.H34   2003
371.93—dc21   2002156491

12 11 10 09 08 07 06 05 04 03   12 11 10 9 8 7 6 5 4 3 2 1

This book is dedicated to the students who graduated from the School Psychology Program at Minot State University from 1993 to 2003. Each of them contributed to the insights shared in this book and the inspiration to write it. Being their mentors enriched our lives immeasurably. We thank them.

We would also like to express our appreciation to the many classroom teachers and special educators with whom we have worked in the K–12 public schools in South Dakota, Minnesota, and North Dakota. Several of them will read vignettes that describe children they worked with, and they will smile. These individuals continue to make a difference for children.

Educating

OPPOSITIONAL

AND DEFIANT

CHILDREN

Acknowledgments

Several colleagues were kind enough to read early drafts of this book and make comments and observations that improved the manuscript. Paul Markel made insightful suggestions on Chapters 1 and 2. John Hoover read the first half of the book and suggested changes that enhanced the book's appeal to a wider audience. Ernie Bantam read much of the original manuscript and made suggestions and comments that kept us faithful to ourselves and to the time-hewn beliefs about children that the three of us share. Charles Jonassaint worked with uncommon dedication to search various aspects of the literature and write the first draft about social skills streaming. We thank them.

We are also indebted to the excellent librarians at Minot State University. In particular, Patti Hunt, Dave Iverson, and Jane LaPlant were always ready to patiently provide desperately needed assistance at hysteric moments. We are indebted to them.

1

Understanding Oppositional Children

A Classroom Incident

"Justin," the teacher directed, "stop playing with your crayon and get back to work." Without even giving the teacher a glance, Justin rolled his crayon down his desk and squealed in delight as it fell to the floor.

Noticing the teacher's exasperation, the classroom aide, Mrs. Johnson, put her hand out and pleaded, "Justin, won't you please give me your crayon?" Justin threw the crayon at Mrs. Johnson, striking her in the forehead.

"Justin!" the teacher exclaimed. "That is enough! Mrs. Johnson," the teacher said to her aide, "take Justin to the office."

When Mrs. Johnson arrived at the office with Justin in tow, the secretary reached for the phone. "Call his mother?" she rhetorically queried. Before Mrs. Johnson could nod her head, Justin pulled out of her grasp, knocked over a chair, and, with the aide in close pursuit, ran back to his classroom. Seeing the commotion, the principal abruptly ended her phone call and came to help.

Schools are seeing more and more children like Justin. They are variously called oppositional-defiant, antisocial, conduct disordered, behaviorally disordered, or severely emotionally disturbed. Whatever the label, these children have common characteristics. They do not listen to directives from adults; they are openly defiant; and, if pushed, they are apt to become aggressive. Twenty years ago most educators had never heard of children who were categorized as being oppositional-defiant, but today many teachers have such a child in their classroom. The recent appearance of so many schoolchildren who are oppositional and defiant makes people wonder whether the prevalence of this condition is increasing. The question has two answers: "No, not really" and "Yes, it really is."

The "No, not really" response is valid because, to a certain extent, the increase simply reflects a change in terminology. Characterizing a child's behavior as oppositional-defiant did not become commonplace until after 1980, the year that the *Diagnostic and Statistical Manual of Mental Disorders* first mentioned the diagnosis of Oppositional Defiant Disorder (ODD) and described the behavioral characteristics associated with it.[1] Previously, children who displayed these behaviors were given other labels. Psychologists and psychiatrists once said these children had Explosive Personality Disorder; teachers referred to the children as disobedient and unruly; and the neighbors called them spoiled brats. The increase in the number of children diagnosed as having oppositional-defiant behaviors is due in part to the appearance in 1980 of a new, more descriptive diagnostic label, and, in that sense, the perceived increase is akin to putting old vinegar into new bottles.

The "Yes, it really is" response can claim widespread statistical evidence. Youth violence in the United States has increased dramatically in the past 20 years.[2] Today schools are dealing with levels of aggression that were unheard of only two decades ago. The headline grabbers include Jonesboro, Arkansas; Springfield, Oregon; and Littleton, Colorado; but the daily incidents of noncompliance, defiance, and aggression by children in schools that go unreported by the media are burgeoning. As Chicken Little might say, "It's everywhere, it's everywhere!" Indeed, from 1976 to 1986 the number of emotionally disturbed children in schools increased 32 percent,[3] and a large-scale study done in the idyllic setting of rural Vermont found that 20 percent of the preschool children in day care displayed frequent aggression.[4]

Staub believes that this pandemic of aggression arises out of social conditions that typify the United States.[5] Specifically, the number of families headed by single mothers has increased 25 percent since 1990.[6] In 1999, 33 percent of children were born to unwed mothers; 42 percent of all children under the age of 6 were living in or near poverty; and 27 percent of all children were living with a single parent, usually a mother.[7] Research has convincingly shown that single parents and parents living in poverty are more likely to use harsh, inconsistent parenting practices, and their children are more likely to be noncompliant, defiant, and aggressive.[8,9]

Staub contends that children who experience neglect, rejection, harsh discipline, and a lack of nurturing develop pent-up anger. Inwardly primed to explode, they do not have to look far to see aggression used as a means for getting even or getting what they want. Violence is a common feature of television programs. Even seemingly benign cartoons such as "Road Runner" portray violent acts, such as Wile E. Coyote getting revenge by rolling a boulder off a cliff onto the indomitable beeping bird. It has been estimated that by age 10 the average child has witnessed 12,000 acts of violence on television. Of more concern, research has shown that when children, particularly boys, see violence modeled on television, they become more aggressive.[10,11] A case in point is a study about the effects of television on the children in a small rural town in Canada that the investigators dubbed Notel. Two years after television was introduced in Notel, the amount of physical violence among children increased 160 percent.[12] Even more sobering, researchers have found that the amount and the type of violence that boys viewed on television at age 8 predicted the seriousness of the crimes they committed by age 30,[4] and that viewing violence on television was a predictive variable among 26-year-old adults, both male and female, who had a criminal record.[13]

Another societal trend that contributes to aggression and noncompliance in young children is day care.[14,15,16] Researchers found that when 4- and 5-year-old children are in day care, their level of salivary cortisol, a hormone secreted when a person is stressed, is markedly higher than when they are in their own homes, and their increase in cortisol parallels an increase in aggression.[17] Researchers have also found that aggression among children in day-care programs is contagious, meaning that when one child is aggressive, the likeli-hood that another child will be aggressive increases.[18] Aggression is particularly contagious if it is successful. That is to say, if Sally watches Joe use aggression to get something he wants, Sally is likely to imitate Joe. Also, aggression is likely to be contagious when it is used against another child. Simply put, children see two kinds of people among their playmates—predators and victims—and most children do not want to be victims.

Possibly more important than the increased aggression seen in children who attend day care is the increase in their noncompliance. In *Language and Cognition*, A. R. Luria explains the development of self-control, which he calls volitional behavior.[19] Luria describes the mother-child bond as the seed from which springs preschool children's ability to have behavior-regulating thought. An infant, according to Luria, is biologically primed to pay particular attention to its mother's voice. For example, when a hungry infant is at its mother's breast, the child will instantly stop sucking if the mother merely whispers. As the infant gets older, the mother uses language to draw the child's atten-tion to certain objects in the environment. For example, the mother asks expectantly, "Where is the cup?" And the child's gaze goes toward the cup. The mother's words direct and control the child's motor act. Next, developmentally speaking, children acquire language and use it just as their mother did, to direct and control their own motor acts. So, walking up to a stove, a 2-year-old says to herself, "Hot. Don't touch," and she pulls her arm back. Finally, in the last stage, children's external speech, or self-talk, is internalized, becomes automatic, and takes over from the mother the function of regulating behavior.

Of course, in order for the child to acquire behavior-regulating thought, the mother's language must be reliable and meaningful. For example, if the mother often asks, "Where is the cup?" and there is no cup, the child stops paying attention to the mother's speech because it does not convey accurate, meaningful information. This breakdown in accuracy of meaning happens frequently in day care. There, the supervising adult may be monitoring as many as six chil-dren, and when the adult says, "Get the cup," six children stop what they are doing to look around for the cup. But perhaps only one child sees a cup. For the other five children, the adult's information is not accurate. Soon they learn to disregard the adult's directives. When the language component of the adult-child bond is dysfunctional, the child learns to ignore instructions from adults; furthermore, the child probably does not develop the inner language that is important for self-control.

 Key Concept

The mother-child bond is the crucible in which children learn compliance and self-control.

Children acquire various components of language during certain developmental windows. They learn to hear the phonemes in their native language by age 1. If they have certain hearing problems, such as chronic fluid in the middle ear, or are not exposed to those phonemes during this critical window, they will, for the rest of their lives, have difficulty hearing phonemes.[20] Chomsky provides another example of a critical window for specific aspects of language.[21] He suggests that for a critical period of their lives, young children are neurologically programmed to learn the rules for putting words together in a certain order to make sentences; but if they reach age 5 without learning these rules, they will always, regardless of the number of hours of speech therapy, speak in tightly scripted, unnatural, simple sentences. It is plausible that children who fail to develop behavior-regulating thought between the critical ages of 1 and 3 are destined to have lifelong problems with self-control.

A Challenge for Educators

In the classroom, oppositional-defiant children are a challenge. They refuse to follow directions. They do not respect other students' property, and they often threaten people's safety. When the teacher attempts to set limits, these children model insolence and rebellion for the entire class. They tip over desks, swear at the teacher, and run out of the room. Although it seems that teachers shouldn't have to put up with this behavior, they do. Under the maxim of educating the child in the least restrictive setting, the courts demand it.

Educators have faced other difficult challenges. In 1975, the Federal Education for All Handicapped Children Act (P.L. 94-142) required schools to provide an appropriate education for children with any disability that affects learning. Meeting that challenge was not easy. Some thought children with learning disabilities could not be educated or served in a public school setting, but they were. In retrospect, it is clear that when educators acquired the skills to teach *all* children, everyone benefited—the children, the family, and society. But quite possibly, educators benefited the most. They became even better teachers.

Now, it is children with oppositional-defiant behaviors who present a challenge to educators. These children are especially difficult because they often probe to find a chink in a teacher's emotional armor and, finding one, run a skewer through it. Not all educators are ready for this challenge. When the child loses control of his or her emotions, many educators lose control of theirs. When the child pushes the limits, the educator, feeling threatened, lays down the law. As the child increasingly behaves like a convict, the teacher takes on the role of the prison warden, strictly enforcing the rules and swiftly doling out the consequences. Both the child and the teacher lose in the ensuing power struggle.

 Key Concept

Educating children who have oppositional-defiant behaviors requires the highest level of emotional maturity.

It takes the highest level of emotional maturity to successfully educate noncompliant, oppositional children. Regardless of the child's behavior, the teacher must always value the child. Without fail, the child must feel emotionally and physically safe in the teacher's presence. To become this type of caregiver, the educator must have hope.

Hope comes from understanding, and understanding comes from empathy; but when teaching oppositional-defiant children, empathy does not come easily.

Normal Noncompliance Versus Abnormal Behavior Development

Isn't noncompliance in young children normal? Yes—up to a point. Most 2-year-old children have occasional temper tantrums and are sometimes downright noncompliant. Some children retain these characteristics through age 3. This early bout of defiance and oppositional behavior is not worrisome; it is an integral part of establishing a self-identity. At that age, learning to resist and even oppose the will of others is part of normal development. It's healthy. However, if the noncompliance is too intense, too frequent, or lasts longer than is developmentally appropriate, it impedes the child's social and intellectual development. Such behavior becomes pathological.

But won't children outgrow their aggressive behavior? Unfortunately, in many cases the answer is no. Second only to intelligence, the propensity toward aggressive behavior is a child's single most stable trait.[22,23] Children who display a difficult temperament at 6 months of age elicit, by age 2, more negative interactions from their mothers.[24] Restlessness at age 3 is associated with antisocial behavior at age 8.[25] Children who display short attention spans and volatile emotions as preschoolers demonstrate antisocial behavior at age 8.[26] Difficulty getting along with preschool peers is the single best predictor of antisocial behaviors at age 11.[27,28] And having a socialized conduct disorder during adolescence is the best predictor of criminality as an adult.[29] Early, well-established patterns of aggressive behavior do not tend to go away.[30]

  Key Concept

Early, well-established patterns of aggression in children often become a lifelong disorder.

A key to whether oppositional behavior will become a lifelong pattern is the presence of another psychological disorder. Attention Deficit Hyperactivity Disorder (ADHD) is a condition that commonly occurs in conjunction with oppositional behaviors. About 30 percent of the children with oppositional-defiant behaviors also have ADHD,[31] and any child who is both oppositional and has attention problems is at particular risk for a lifelong pattern of aggression.[32] When these children become adolescents, their world expands. Many of them extend their propensity toward defiance and aggression from their home and classroom to the community. They shoplift, fight with unfamiliar peers, skip school, and engage in vandalism. When their behavior comes to the attention of the mental health profession, they are diagnosed as having Conduct Disorder (CD).

Conduct Disorder is a pattern of aggressive, antisocial behavior that affects the public, such as stealing and vandalism. There are two types of Conduct Disorder: undersocialized CD, in which the adolescent engages in antisocial behavior alone; and socialized CD, in which the individual acts as part of a group or a gang. Adolescents with socialized CD have the more troublesome outcome. Possibly because of peer pressure, they almost invariably become substance abusers. As young adults, they no longer shoplift; instead, they may break into houses and businesses. They no longer fight with peers, but they may mug strangers to get money for drugs. They don't vandalize cars, but they may steal them. Eventually they acquire the final diagnosis: Antisocial Personality Disorder (APD). Many criminals have APD.[33]

Risk Factors

Three factors put a child at risk for developing a pattern of oppositional-defiant behaviors. The risk factors are (1) an inherently difficult temperament, (2) parents with marginal skills at disciplining and nurturing, and (3) parents under excessive stress.

Temperament

Some children are born with a temperament that makes them hard to parent, and their inherent temperament puts them at risk for developing noncompliant, oppositional, and aggressive behaviors.

Mrs. Larson's Story

"Brandon was my third child," Mrs. Larson related during a parent training session. "I knew even in pregnancy that he was going to be difficult. He was a kicker. When Brandon was born, he came into the world with a loud scream. In the hospital, he was inconsolable. He would nurse for a short period, then lose interest. An hour later he'd be fussing because he was hungry. I couldn't get an hour's worth of sleep. The doctor kept us in the hospital two extra days trying to see if there was something wrong with my baby. He concluded it was just Brandon.

"I enjoyed mothering my other two children, but I have to tell you," Mrs. Larson said, with tears streaming down her face, "I did not enjoy mothering Brandon. Nothing comforted him. I remember picking up my other children as infants. Their eyes lit up, they smiled, they enjoyed being held. Not Brandon. When I picked him up, he squirmed and whined. It got so I picked him up only when he needed to be fed or changed. I suppose that was bad of me," she said, crying again.

Regaining her composure, Mrs. Larson continued. "When Brandon was little, I passed his belligerence off as a bad case of the terrible 2s. But by the time he was 4, I realized he was a snot. I'm sorry to say that," Mrs. Larson confessed, looking around to gauge people's reactions, "but he was. My parents live only 40 miles away, but they stopped coming by and we didn't get invited to their house very often.

"I thought things would get better when Brandon went to school. They didn't. Brandon was in kindergarten only three weeks when the teacher called me in for a conference. She said Brandon was not ready for school. She wanted me to hold him out another year. I did. But the next year didn't go any better. He got into lots of fights. Since he was bigger than the other kids, the school decided the fights were Brandon's fault. The principal told me that I wasn't disciplining Brandon right at home or he wouldn't have problems at school."

Increasingly, evidence suggests that a difficult temperament such as Brandon's has genetic roots. As previously mentioned, oppositional-defiant behavior is often accompanied by ADHD, a disorder with clearly established genetic links. Boys are four times more likely than girls to have ODD,[28] which suggests that ODD is either sex-linked or sex-limited. Also, ODD is more prevalent in children who have at least one parent who has a mood disorder, ADHD, problems with substance abuse, or an Antisocial Personality Disorder—all of which have solid evidence of a genetic pattern.[34] Finally, studies of adopted twins provide additional evidence. Adopted twins, even if they were separated and raised by different parents, are at increased risk of becoming criminals if one of their biological parents has a criminal record.[35]

The genetic component expresses itself through biochemical anomalies. Boys with undersocialized CD show markedly higher levels of dopamine-beta-hydroxylase (DBH), an enzyme necessary for abating the effects of the emotion-arousing hormone adrenalin.[36] Also, adults and children known to be particularly impulsive and aggressive have low levels of epinephrine, an enzyme that reduces serotonin levels,[37] a neurotransmitter that modulates mood, emotions, sleep, and appetite. High levels of serotonin are associated with aggression. Finally, low levels of monoamine oxidase (MAO), an iron-containing enzyme that modulates a person's response to arousal-producing stimuli, are consistently found in people who are impulsive.[38]

Biochemistry probably played a role in the behavior of Justin, the child in the anecdote at the start of this chapter. Justin didn't intentionally abandon his art project in order to roll a crayon down his desk. It just happened. It might have happened to any student. But when it happened to Justin, the crayon became the dominant stimulus, and it grabbed his attention. Another child's behavior inhibition system (BIS) would have kicked in and told him to get back on task. But Justin's frontal lobes do not process the glucose necessary to generate behavior-regulating thoughts. For him, the most salient stimulus impinging upon him at the moment "owns" him. Biochemistry can help us look at Justin's behavior with greater understanding.

The Classroom Incident Revisited

"Wow!" Justin said to himself. "That was cool!" And he again rolled the crayon down his desk. Mrs. Smith directed Justin to stop playing with the crayon and get back to work. For an instant, Mrs. Smith's directive was the dominant stimulus. But her directive was as ephemeral as the sound waves that carried it to Justin's ear. The feel of the crayon in his hand was more immediate, durable, and demanding. He let go of the crayon and squealed in delight as it fell to the floor.

At this point, Mrs. Johnson, the aide, put her hand on Justin's. Her hand was a lasting, dominant stimulus, and he paid attention to it. But Justin's brain has low levels of 5-HIAA, which means he is aggressive. When Mrs. Johnson said, "Justin, won't you please give me your crayon?" he complied, but with a tinge of aggression. Justin threw the crayon at her.

Mrs. Smith then told her aide to take Justin to the office. Another child in a similar situation would have calmed down between the classroom and the office, but not Justin. He does not have the DBH necessary to abate the effects of the adrenalin urging him to fight or take flight. In the office, Justin saw the secretary phoning his home. Justin knew that his stepdad would be coming to get him. At this point, his biochemistry was in sync with his experience. He knew that when he got home his stepdad would spank him with a belt and lock him in his room. Justin ran back to his refuge, the classroom.

Parenting Skills

The second risk factor that increases the likelihood of developing oppositional-defiant behaviors is having parents with marginal, inconsistent discipline practices.[34] Patterson believes that children with these behaviors are raised by parents who inadvertently but almost invariably reward them for being noncompliant and defiant.[39] He developed the Coercive Hypothesis to explain the dynamic. The Coercive Hypothesis begins when a parent asks the child to do something. The child refuses to comply. With rising emotions, the parent repeats the request, and the child responds with abrasive defiance. To avoid a stressful and unpleasant confrontation, the parent withdraws the request. Of course, withdrawing the request rewards the child for being noncompliant and defiant, and it thereby increases the frequency and the intensity of future problematic behavior.

In the home, the Coercive Hypothesis might look like this:

The Struggle

"It's time for bed," Justin's mother said.

"No!" Justin yelled, running down the hall.

"Right now," the mother ordered, running after him. Catching Justin by the arm, she shook him. "Get in bed right now, and I mean it!"

Justin kicked her and lunged to get away. He ran into the living room and lay down in front of the television. Mom knew that if she just let him be, Justin would settle down, watch TV, and soon fall asleep. But if she repeated her demand, Justin would throw a tantrum again. After a long day, she was not up for a big battle over such a "small" issue.

Although Patterson's analysis of the dynamics of oppositional-defiant behavior has much to recommend, it also raises concerns. The Coercive Hypothesis does not give adequate weight to the role played by the child's temperament. As Urie Bronfenbrenner points out, the parent-child relationship is a two-way dynamic.[40] The parent affects how the child behaves, but how the child behaves also affects the parent. The Coercive Hypothesis is also cause for concern if it mistakenly reinforces the prevalent perception that parents are the root cause of the child's behavior problems. Blaming the parents does nothing to promote a solution. Instead, blaming the parents drives them away from professionals who might be able to help. Blaming the parents for the child's behavior also ignores the fact that most of these parents have raised other children who behave normally.

   Key Concept

Don't blame the parent for the child's behavior.

Stress

The third risk factor for oppositional-defiant behavior is a high level of parent stress.[41] Our clinic asked mothers of oppositional children to complete the Parent Stress Index (PSI).[42] The composite PSI of nearly every mother was at the 99th percentile, which is the highest level of stress the instrument will measure. The lowest PSI score recorded by any mother was 95, meaning that this mother, a speech therapist with a master's degree, felt more stress than 95 out of 100 mothers.

External Stress. Mothers of oppositional children are particularly apt to have high levels of external stress. Many of them are single parents who either live on welfare or have unsatisfying, low-paying jobs.[9] In the task of parenting, they have no assistance and no relief.

A Mother with Three Strikes

Gloria, a divorced mother of a 7-year-old girl, Sally, was the embodiment of external stress. Sally's father, Joe, was very committed to his daughter. Although Joe lived 60 miles away, he came to Gloria's home every Friday evening so that he could take Sally for the weekend.

Gloria was a full-time college student. She also worked two part-time jobs. Every minute of her day was scheduled with military precision. Gloria woke her daughter at 6:15 a.m. sharp. Sally had 30 minutes to dress, eat breakfast, brush her teeth, and comb her hair. Gloria left Sally with the sitter at 6:45 so that she could get to her first job by 7:00. From the sitter's house, Sally went to school. After school, she went back to the sitter's house until her mother picked her up at 9:10 p.m. At home, Sally took a bath, set out her school clothes, and was in bed by 9:30.

Sally was particularly fussy about her clothes. They had to look just right, and sometimes she changed outfits several times before she was ready to go out the door. But it was crucial for Gloria to get to work on time. If Sally got behind schedule, Gloria sometimes carried her kicking and screaming to the car. Out of frustration, Gloria sometimes resorted to the ultimate threat: "Get dressed in the clothes we laid out or you can't go with your father this weekend!"

Internal Stress. Stress can also be created by internal issues. Because mothers play the dominant role in parenting, research on the stress experienced by parents of children with oppositional-defiant behaviors has primarily focused on mothers. This research shows that mothers of children who are oppositional and defiant are at increased risk for marital stress.[43] Many of them report that they are dissatisfied with their marital relationships. The lower the mother's marital satisfaction, the more likely she is to have negative perceptions of her children, to make unrealistic and poorly executed requests of them, and to discipline harshly and inconsistently.[44] From the child's perspective, the only thing worse than having an unhappily married mother is having an unmarried mother. Unmarried mothers are especially prone to be critical of their child, to make harshly worded demands, and to use corporal punishment. Not surprisingly, their children are particularly apt to be noncompliant, defiant, and aggressive.[9,45]

Internal stress can also be due to psychiatric illness. Commonly, the mothers of oppositional children are clinically depressed or have some other mood disorder.[46] Socially, they tend to be withdrawn and isolated.[45] Substance abuse is often a problem for one or both of the parents, and the fathers frequently have ADHD[47] and sometimes Antisocial Personality Disorder as well.[48]

Simply stated, stress makes parenting more difficult. This is called the amplifying effect, meaning that stress leads to a marked decline in an adult's ability to parent in a positive way. More importantly, excessive levels of stress change parenting from a pleasure into drudgery.

The Development of the Oppositional Child

The presence of any one of the three risk factors puts a child at risk for developing oppositional-defiant behaviors. However, as the number of risk factors increases, the likelihood of the child developing oppositional-defiant behavior increases. When all three risk factors come together, the child almost cannot avoid becoming oppositional and defiant.

Clinical experience suggests that once a child develops a pattern of oppositional-defiant behaviors, an additional factor comes into play—the child's emotional response to failure. Most children who do not succeed, whether at reading or developing relationships, make attempts to adapt to their failure. Among other reactions, oppositional children seem to develop heightened levels of aggression. Unable to get their needs met through positive, socially appropriate behavior, they become frustrated. Frustration leads to aggression, and aggression often works. Children who do not have the social skills for joining a group on the playground learn to bully their way into the game. These children also have trouble reading the subtle social cues necessary to build relationships, so they save face by rejecting other people before other people reject them. Because they have problems predicting the course of events, they defiantly enact their own agenda. When the failure persona gets well established, it is difficult to get close enough to these defiant children to help them. However, it can be done. This book explains how.

2

Why Commonly Used Approaches Often Fail

Every seasoned educator has taught several children who were
oppositional and defiant. Even though years may have passed, the
teacher can still vividly recall these children. If asked to explain their
behavior, the teacher could bring the disorder to life by sharing the
children's stories.

Here are the stories of three such students. In subsequent chapters,
we suggest techniques that can be used to develop programs and
strategies for successfully serving children like these in the classroom.

Three Stories

Justin

His Family: Justin, age 5, lived with his mother, Mrs. Juliette Jennings,
and his stepdad, Tom. Justin was one of three children from Mrs. Jennings's previous marriage. The two older children lived with their biological father in California. Juliette had recently married Tom.
According to Mrs. Jennings, Tom was an alcoholic. She claimed that
when Tom was drunk, he was physically and emotionally abusive to
Justin. She tried not to leave Justin home alone with Tom, but sometimes she had no choice. Mrs. Jennings worked as an aide in a nursing
home. Her 8-hour shift changed every two weeks, requiring her to work,

over a six-week period, all 24 hours of the day. Mr. Jennings, a fire fighter, worked three consecutive days and then was off for four days.

Justin's Behavior at Home: Because of his parents' varying work schedules, Justin had no routine at home. He ate, slept, and played whenever he wanted. If his mother attempted to set an expectation, Justin became abrasively defiant. During the past year, he had even started giving his mother ultimatums: "Buy me a RoboCop or I am going to stay up all night watching my videos!"

School: Two weeks after Mrs. Jennings enrolled Justin in kindergarten, the principal informed her that Justin was socially immature and not ready for school. Mrs. Jennings then placed Justin in day care. Within two months, Justin was unwelcome at every day-care program in town. The family moved across town to get into a different attendance area, and Mrs. Jennings enrolled Justin in a half-day, five-days-a-week kindergarten program. If Mrs. Jennings was working the morning shift, Justin was expected to get himself to school. After school, he was expected to prepare lunch for himself and play in the house until his mother came home at 2:30.

For the first two weeks, Mrs. Jennings did not hear from the school. She was relieved when Justin told her everything was going well. Then one day the principal phoned. "Justin is not having a good day at school today," she reported. "You need to come get him and take him home." Mrs. Jennings left work to respond to this school "emergency." Soon the school was calling daily, usually at about 10 o'clock. Mrs. Jennings's supervisor at work told her that if she continued signing out, he would be forced to release her.

In desperation, Mrs. Jennings turned to her husband for help. He was often home when the phone call came from school. However, after Tom retrieved Justin, he often spanked Justin with a belt and locked him in his bedroom until noon. In Tom's mind, he was doing the right thing. He felt that Justin needed to be punished for his misbehavior at school and should not be allowed to play during the time he was supposed to be in school.

Justin's Behavior in School: When he was behaving well in school, Justin was charming. He had silky black hair, long dark eyelashes, and good looks. He was a peer leader, but a negative one. In an instant, he could have half a dozen kids following him into trouble. Justin entered kindergarten reading at the 3rd grade level. Academically speaking, he had nothing to learn in kindergarten.

In the classroom, Justin behaved just as he behaved at home. He ran the show. It never occurred to him that his teacher, Mrs. Smith, was in charge. When Mrs. Smith gave directives, Justin often ignored them. If she insisted on compliance, Justin became verbally abusive. If she used a physical prompt, he pulled away. If Mrs. Smith persisted, he hit or kicked her.

An Analysis of Justin's Situation

Justin was past the point of being described as a child with oppositional and defiant behaviors. He was so oppositional and, when pushed, instantly aggressive toward both peers and adults that he had been diagnosed by a pediatric psychiatrist as having Oppositional Defiant Disorder (ODD). Mrs. Jennings was saddled with a minimum-wage, shift-work job. Privately she said she wanted to divorce Tom but couldn't because Tom owned the house the family lived in. If she divorced her husband, she and Justin would have no place to live. Mrs. Jennings knew that she was too often leaving Justin unsupervised, but she could not afford sitters.

In these circumstances, Justin was doing the best he could to raise himself. Each day, he got himself out of bed, dressed, and went to school. He developed the necessary survival skills to look after himself for long periods. The hallmarks of his survival skills were independence and self-reliance. Unfortunately, these traits set him up to clash with adults who expected a 5-year-old child to take directions and comply with classroom rules.

Cassandra

Her Family: Cassandra, age 10, lived with her unmarried mother, Mrs. Coleman. Cassandra had an older half-sister who lived in a foster home in another town. Mrs. Coleman was unemployed, but she received long-term welfare as a result of being diagnosed with Generalized Anxiety Disorder, which made it difficult for her to work.

Cassandra's Behavior at Home: When Cassandra was 4 years old, Mrs. Coleman took her to see a physician's assistant, who diagnosed Cassandra as having ADHD and prescribed Ritalin. From that point on, Cassandra was usually on one medication or another for behavior control. Nonetheless, Mrs. Coleman found it difficult to manage Cassandra at home. Mrs. Coleman reported that Cassandra behaved best when they stuck to a schedule, but any time the schedule was disrupted, which was common, Cassandra became difficult to control.

School: Cassandra had struggled in kindergarten. She was "socially" promoted to the 1st grade because the educators felt that Cassandra needed more time in a structured environment. With a lot of one-to-one help, she barely managed, according to her teachers, to get to 3rd grade. In the 3rd grade, she often did not complete assignments. Despite a great deal of teacher help and curriculum modifications, Cassandra's academic skills in reading and math were below grade level. Yet the teacher, Ms. Jones, reported that Cassandra did well in class discussions based on general knowledge or information presented visually.

Cassandra's Behavior at School: On the days when Cassandra could not stay on task, finish desk assignments, or follow classroom rules, she was impulsive both in action and with words. According to Ms. Jones, "she talked without thinking," often disrupting the class by blurting out whatever she was thinking. Most cooperative learning tasks broke down because Cassandra started "name-calling." Days like these often ended with Cassandra in tears. Ms. Jones wondered whether, on those days, Cassandra had been given her medication.

Even on days when Cassandra was not impulsive and, in Ms. Jones's words, "squirmy," she was typically noncompliant. When asked to do academic tasks, Cassandra often announced, "I'm not doing that," or, if she didn't publicly announce her defiance, she sat at her desk, folded her arms across her chest, and glared at Ms. Jones. When Ms. Jones came to help, Cassandra would not interact with her or even explain the problem. In addition, she was highly demanding of Ms. Jones's attention, typically interrupting Ms. Jones when the teacher was working with other students and Cassandra was supposed to be doing independent work. During these times, Cassandra made an average of two attempts every five minutes to divert Ms. Jones's attention by walking up to wherever the teacher was and, regardless of what Ms. Jones was doing, saying something like, "Help me" or "I can't do this" or "Is this right?"

On the positive side, Cassandra liked and responded well to praise.

An Analysis of Cassandra's Situation

Cassandra probably had ADHD, and it seemed like many of the problems she was having in the classroom could be mitigated by working cooperatively with Mrs. Coleman and the physician to have the right medication reliably administered. Cassandra's positive reaction to praise and attention suggested that her noncompliance and oppositional behaviors might be triggered by academic problems. A comprehensive psycho-educational evaluation was recommended.

Harry

His Family: Harry, age 12, was part of a blended family. There were Dad's kids, Mom's kids, and the couple's new baby. Mr. Weston, Harry's biological father, was a middle-level administrator. Mrs. Weston was a speech therapist. Both of the Westons' divorced spouses lived in the same city. Harry had an older sister, Rebecca, who remained in the custody of her biological mother, though she periodically spent time at the Weston home.

Mrs. Weston had two children from her previous marriage. Although her former husband had custody of the children, they were at the Westons' home every other weekend and every other holiday. This meant that four children rotated in and out of the Weston home, leaving chaos in their wake. Harry stayed with his biological mother when things got too tense in the Weston home. When things got tense at his biological mother's house, Harry, by his own choice, returned to the Weston home.

Harry's Behavior at Home: By the time Harry was in 6th grade, the Westons had more or less stopped parenting him. They were resigned to living in the chaos that Harry created in their home. Their house, although relatively new, was severely damaged. Every wall had gaping holes in the sheetrock. Doors hung suspended on hinges that had been jerked partway out of the wall. Several cupboard doors were missing. Broken windows were patched with cardboard and duct tape. Harry had inflicted all of this damage. Anytime he lost his temper, something got broken. Of course, Harry lost his temper anytime his dad attempted to set an expectation or impose a consequence. Now, Harry had won. His parents made only one demand of him. They expected Harry to stay out of their bedroom.

School: Harry's school career started without any major problems. Except for difficulties in completing tasks, following directions, and listening, he was successful in kindergarten and 1st grade. In 2nd grade, the teacher held several conferences with Harry's parents about their son's behavior, but nothing changed. In 3rd grade, Harry's grades began to slide, and referrals to the principal's office increased. In 4th grade, Harry was diagnosed with ADHD and placed on medication. He took the medication for two weeks but then refused to take it any longer. By 6th grade, Harry was failing most of his classes.

Harry's Behavior at School: Harry's mantra was "I don't want to do any schoolwork, and they can't make me." It was both a promise and a threat. If a teacher tried to get Harry to do any schoolwork, he went on a campaign to make life miserable for that teacher, both in and out of school. On the positive side, if a teacher gave an assignment but expressed no expectation of Harry, he often did the work. However, many completed assignments got lost before they made it to the teacher's desk.

An Analysis of Harry's Situation

Harry was born with a temperament that put him at risk to become oppositional and defiant. He was easily distracted and instantly detonated. To avoid Harry's outbursts, his parents made no demands on him, but in the process, no one helped him learn to control his temper so that he could be a responsible member of a functional family. Now, at age 12, Harry was no longer a child with ODD. Because of vandalism of public property, truancy from school, and shoplifting, he was an adolescent with Conduct Disorder. Because of his temperament and his inability to conform to the expectations of any group, he was a loner.

What *Not* to Do with Students Like Justin, Cassandra, and Harry

Children with behaviors like Justin's, Cassandra's, and Harry's are a challenge in the classroom. Anyone who has the magic potion for transforming children with oppositional and defiant behaviors into "normal" children is not sharing it. The literature suggests that rearing and educating a child who is chronically oppositional and defiant are a matter of doing the best job possible. There is no cure, but there are specific techniques and skills that help. At least part of the answer lies in knowing what *not* to do.

Applied Behavior Analysis

Behavior Modification, or Applied Behavior Analysis (ABA) as it is now called after a few conceptual changes, is a commonly used approach for guiding children's behavior. ABA is based on the principle that reinforcement and punishment control behavior. That is, if a response is reinforced, its rate increases.[1] If a response is punished, its rate decreases.[a] The straightforward application of these principles works for 95 percent of children, and their behavior responds readily to rewards and consequences. However, clinicians are increasingly recognizing that the behavior of children who, by temperament, are oppositional, impulsive, easily distracted, and inattentive is not particularly responsive to systematically delivered rewards and punishment.

The Dull Pencil

As he distributed a math worksheet to his 2nd graders, Mr. Burke said, "Take out a pencil." Donald opened his desk and got his pencil. The lead was broken. While Mr. Burke explained the directions for completing the worksheet, Donald went to the pencil sharpener. He whirled and whirled the handle of the pencil sharpener, grinding an inch off his pencil. When his arm grew tired, Donald looked at the pencil. It was sharp. Suddenly, a shiny object in the wastepaper basket grabbed his attention. Like a magnet, it drew Donald's hand into the wastepaper basket. It was a gum wrapper. Unwrapping it, Donald's fingers found a wet glob of chewed gum.

Holding his sticky fingers in front of him, Donald went to the sink. He turned on the water to wet his hands. Seeing the soap dispenser, he pushed it vigorously. The soap squirted all over his hands and onto the counter. Leaving the water running full force and splashing out of the sink, Donald pulled down some towels to wipe up the soap. Meanwhile, the floor was getting drenched. As Donald stepped back to the sink, his feet slid out from under him and he fell. When Donald landed on his bottom, a sharp object poked him in the rear. He reached for the thing that had poked him. Retrieving it, he saw that the tip of the pencil was broken. Leaving the water running and holding the pencil in front of him, Donald headed back to the pencil sharpener.

From Mr. Burke's perspective, Donald had been thoughtlessly disruptive. Intercepting Donald en route to the pencil sharpener, Mr. Burke said, "Donald, the rule is that students stay at their desk when I am talking to the class. I'm putting a checkmark after your name. That is your second checkmark today. You'll stay in at recess."

If Donald had intentionally disrupted Mr. Burke's teaching, the consequence of missing recess would affect his behavior. However, nothing about Donald's behavior had been intentional. He had simply followed the stimulus at the end of his nose from one disrupting activity to the next. Staying in at recess will do nothing to help him make a better decision next time. To paraphrase Bob Dylan, the American folk singer, "You can't change what you can't understand."

Types of Consequences in the ABA Model

Punishment. Because punishment, by definition, reduces the probability of a response recurring, it would seem to be exactly what children who are noncompliant and oppositional need. After all, what could be better than a reduction in these troublesome behaviors? Examples of punishment techniques and their usefulness in reducing negative behavior abound in the literature. The principal techniques are administration of an aversive stimulus[2] (such as giving a person electric shock treatment for doing a self-injurious behavior), over-correction[3] (acts of restitution or repetitive acts of "doing it right"), response cost[4] (removing a person's positive reinforcers as a consequence for a behavior), and time-out[5] (temporarily removing the individual from an environment with reinforcers to an environment where there is no opportunity to earn reinforcement).

Using punishment on children who are oppositional and possibly impulsive indicates a flawed assumption. It assumes that the child considered the consequences for the behavior, carefully weighed the chances of getting caught, and then deliberately engaged in the inappropriate behavior. In truth, children with temperament-related problems give little thought to the consequences of their behavior. Most of their inappropriate behavior stems from either an unpremeditated impulse, or it is propelled by so much emotion that the outburst is beyond their conscious control. In either case, punishing the behavior does not help change the behavior. Punishment is also problematic for children who have adopted the oppositional persona because they often are willing to defiantly absorb severe punishment rather than "give in."

Ignoring the Behavior. A response that occurs at a high rate is generally somehow rewarded. If the reward is removed, the response often ceases, a process that is called extinction.[6] In the classroom, the application of this principle of ABA is called planned ignoring.[7] Ignoring works for many children. For example, Jack, a 2nd grader, frequently pulls Karen's braids. Jack loves it when Karen turns around and says, "Don't do that!" Her attention rewards him for pulling her hair. However, if Jack pulled Karen's braids five consecutive times and she didn't respond, he probably would stop pulling her braids and would search for a different, hopefully more socially acceptable way to get her attention.

It could be argued that Donald disrupted the classroom to get Mr. Burke's attention. Therefore, if Mr. Burke ignored the disruptions, Donald would no longer receive reinforcement. He would, according to the principle of extinction, stop the disruptive behaviors. Not a chance. Donald wasn't seeking anyone's attention. He will never notice that he is being ignored. Ignoring seldom works with children who are oppositional and defiant. They have to look in the rearview mirror to see that their behavior affected others. Understanding that is only achieved by hindsight has little impact on the next impulsive behavior.

Rewards. If a response occurs at a low rate, its frequency will be increased by following the response with a reward.[8] One way to deal with a child who has a problematic behavior is to reward a response that is incompatible with the inappropriate behavior. In Donald's case, he could be rewarded for remaining in his seat while Mr. Burke is talking. A fixed-interval reinforcement schedule is commonly used to increase on-task behavior. For each five-minute period that Donald sits quietly at his desk while Mr. Burke is presenting a lesson, he will receive a token. At the end of the day, Donald can exchange his tokens for something he wants, perhaps an action figure.

For a few hours, Donald will put his heart and soul into earning tokens. He might even go all Monday morning without interrupting Mr. Burke's teaching. Donald will be pleased with himself, and Mr. Burke will be relieved that Donald no longer interrupts him. However, it takes extreme vigilance to control impulsive behaviors, and Donald's success will be short-lived. By Wednesday, Donald will be interrupting Mr. Burke's teaching once again.

A common and erroneous conclusion in this situation is that Donald's success was brief because he did not place a high enough value on the action figure. After all, he has several of them at home. But because a small reward worked for a short time, a big reward should work for a longer time. Donald's parents, wanting to be supportive of the teacher, say that they will reward Donald by taking him to a movie Friday night if he can earn 30 tokens. Again, Monday goes great. Donald interrupts Mr. Burke only once. Tuesday goes okay, but not as well.

By Wednesday, things fall apart. Donald realizes that he will never earn the needed tokens and he quits trying. Not only does he quit trying to earn the movie, but he has also learned not to invest himself in any behavior plan that a teacher might try to implement.

A "token economy system" is the application of the reward principle to an entire system.[9] In an education setting, every child in the classroom earns daily points for good behavior, such as completing worksheets.[10] At the end of the day, "the store is open," and children can trade earned points for items on the shelves.

A Day at the Store

At the start of the day, the teacher took Jason, an oppositional and highly impulsive child, to the store. Hoping to motivate him, she asked him, "What do you want to work for today?" After looking over the various items, Jason decided that he wanted to work for a slick, black toy car. It cost 75 points. The teacher assured Jason that if he did all of his work, he could earn the needed points.

For the first hour, Jason stayed at his desk and did all of his assignments. "How many points did I earn?" he excitedly asked his teacher.

"Fifteen!" she responded. "Way to go."

However, things did not continue to go well for Jason. A packet of math worksheets proved to be too difficult for him. After unsuccessfully attempting three problems, Jason tore up the math sheets. The teacher flashed him "the look" but wisely did not say anything.

During the rest of the day, Jason completed many assignments— more than usual—but not all of them. At the end of the day, he stood impatiently waiting while the teacher tallied his points. "You have 60 points," she announced. Jason started to reach for the car. "No," the teacher said. "You will have to select something else today, Jason. Look on the third shelf. The things there cost 60 points."

"But I want the car!" Jason insisted.

"I'm sorry, Jason. You didn't earn enough points for the car," the teacher soothingly replied. Jason looked longingly at the car. Suddenly he grabbed it and threw it as hard as he could against the wall, breaking it into pieces.

Key Concept

Consequences—positive or negative—have little impact on the behavior of children who have oppositional behaviors with ODD.

For children who have a difficult temperament, a reward that requires control of impulsive behaviors is a cruel hoax. They seldom earn the reward. Eventually, they disengage from the adult who promised the reward. Worse, they start to see themselves as failures. Children with oppositional and defiant behaviors are too impulsive, too much under the control of the dominant stimulus, and too often the victim of their emotions to benefit from a system that requires them to consider the consequence of an action before doing it. They cannot make their behavior serve their best interest.

A Final Caveat

Not all children who display oppositional and defiant behaviors are also so impulsive and inattentive that they cannot predict and understand that inappropriate behaviors will lead to a consequence. Seemingly, children who do not have these additional problems should be amenable to the powerful effects of systematically applied rewards and punishment. However, they are not. These children are resolutely oppositional. Once they reach age 10, most of them resent any attempt by an adult to "control" their behavior, and they actively and forcibly resist all behavior modification plans.

Notes

ªApplied Behavior analysts define punishment as an event that, if it immediately follows a behavior, causes the behavior to decrease in frequency. However, in the classroom, punishment almost invariably means following a response with an aversive stimulus—overcorrection, response cost, or time-out—all designed to make the person think twice about doing that behavior again.

3

Engineering the Child's Environment for Success

Because a reward-consequence paradigm often fails with children who are oppositional and defiant, a more complex approach is needed. In our clinical work in helping oppositional children and their families, we have discovered the importance of arranging the environment to set the child up for success—something that might be called environmental engineering, or manipulating what have been called "the setting events."[1] An example of environmental engineering is the planning done before we first see a child in the clinic. "The intent of these sessions," we tell the parents, "is to teach the child the requisite skills for being able to participate in a nurturing relationship. We will begin by spending a productive hour with the child without eliciting his noncompliance and defiance."

Hearing this, the parents raise their eyebrows in disbelief. "You don't know my kid! It will never happen," they warn.

Well, it does happen. We don't give the child any other choice. Before the child enters the clinic, the environment is meticulously arranged so that we can work for an hour with the child without having to give a single verbal directive. In the early stages of treatment, we avoid verbal directives because they often elicit noncompliance and defiance from these children.

Key Concept

If given a verbal directive, these children often become oppositional and defiant.

We also arrange the environment so that it is difficult for the child to do the wrong thing and the easiest thing for the child to do is the right thing. From the moment the parent relinquishes responsibility of the child, the environment conspires to elicit the child's best behavior.

The Child's Perspective

My mom and I were sitting in a waiting room. A woman came in, introduced herself, and talked a little with me but mostly with my mother. There was nothing for me to do. I was bored. Then a man came out a door. He had a jar of bubbles. He blew one in my direction and gestured for me to break it. I like to break things! So I did. Kneeling down, the man blew some bubbles right over his head, and he beckoned to me to break them. I walked over and broke them. As I broke these bubbles, the man opened the door behind him and started to walk slowly down the hall, still blowing bubbles. He gestured for me to follow and keep breaking bubbles. I looked around for my mom. She was standing right behind me. Just then, the light went off in the waiting room and it got all dark. So I looked at the man, and he blew another bubble for me to break. I broke that one too.

The man walked past an open door and stopped. Behind him was a long, dark hallway. All I could see was a bunch of closed doors. Only one door was open, and that was the one right beside me. There was a light on in the room. The man gestured for me to go into the room. But first I looked around for my mom. She and that woman were right behind me. Mom was smiling. She looked calm. I figured things must be okay. I started to go in the room, and as I did, the man handed me the wand. He wanted me to blow some bubbles.

The environment was engineered so that everything conspired to transition the child from the waiting room to the therapy room without the need for a single verbal directive. Every time the child had to make a decision, the environment worked to make the desired response the easiest thing for the child to do.

 Key Concept

Arrange the child's environment so that the right response is the easiest response.

The therapist held out something of interest to the child and walked slightly ahead of him. Mammals have an innate tendency, called a tropism, to follow things that are going away from them. (Hence, don't run from a mountain lion!) By interest and instinct, the child followed the therapist. To make sure that the child moved in the right direction, two adults positioned themselves behind him. Self-preservation also came into play. The assistant turned off the lights in the waiting room. The child was not apt to run headlong back into a dark room. In the hallway, two stimuli were working to help the child make the right response. The long hallway grew progressively darker. The only light came from a room to the child's immediate right, and that door was open. The child had three options: freeze in place, try to slip past the man standing in front of him and run down a dark hallway, or go into the room and get to blow some bubbles. From the child's perspective, the easiest thing to do was to walk toward the light into the clinic room. (Mammals are heliotropic, meaning they tend to move toward light.) From the clinician's point of view, walking into the clinic room was the desired response. Because the child made the right response, the clinician had an opportunity to subtly acknowledge to the child that he made a good decision. The first and most critical step of relationship building had been taken.

When the environment is skillfully engineered, children can be guided into a correct response without the need for a verbal directive, which is anathema for these children. Environmental engineering also makes it less likely that the child will make a response that is wrong. Children with oppositional dispositions often explode with anger when they are told, even in the most subtle, benign way, that they did something wrong.

 Key Concept

When children with oppositional dispositions are given any indication that they did something wrong, they often become defiant and aggressive.

Just as environmental engineering was useful in the clinic, it is extremely helpful when applied to the classroom. In an educational setting, environmental engineering starts with arranging the child's macroenvironment—the classroom—and ends with arranging the microenvironment—those things right at the end of the child's fingertips. The components of environmental engineering in the classroom are the organization of the classroom, the seating arrangement, the daily schedule, the work structure, the tasks, and additional assistance. Figure 3.1 provides a checklist that educators can use to ensure that these elements have been considered in the plan for dealing with an oppositional child. The following sections discuss these elements in more detail.

Macroenvironment

Organization of the Classroom

Many children profit from an enriched classroom. To achieve this kind of environment, teachers spend hours putting up colorful posters with positive quotations, lining the walls with the students' work, and enlivening the classroom with fish tanks and ant farms. However, children who have attention problems cannot survive in a cluttered, visually "busy" classroom. For them, even the layout and organization of the classroom need to suggest order, structure, and purpose. Initially, meeting the needs of "normal" children for an enriched environment

Figure 3.1
Environmental Engineering Checklist

Classroom

☐ Uncluttered room
☐ Enrichment items strategically placed in the room, possibly in learning centers
☐ Seating arrangement with optimal placement of the child's desk
☐ Child's desk of the right size

Organizational Tools

☐ Daily schedule
    ☐ Object schedule
    ☐ Pic symbol schedule
    ☐ Written word schedule

☐ Work structure
    ☐ Workbaskets
    ☐ Activity boxes
    ☐ Trapper Keeper or three-ring binder
    ☐ Daily worksheet

☐ Tasks
    ☐ At child's developmental or academic level
    ☐ Good visual clarity
    ☐ Clear finish
    ☐ Only one response set per page
    ☐ Extraneous writing and pictures removed

Extra Assistance

☐ Need for a classroom aide
☐ Need for assistance from specialists

seems incompatible with meeting the needs of easily distracted children. However, with care and consideration, educators can meet the learning needs of both groups. Stimulating, enriching activities can be confined to well-defined areas, such as learning centers placed in the back of the classroom. The main part of the classroom—where the teacher provides direct instruction—should be as free of distractions as is feasible. This means no dangling mobiles, no gallery of student artwork, and no similar potential distractions.

Seating Arrangement

A child with attention problems should not be seated next to distracting stimuli. He needs to be seated away from the fish tank, the window, and the door to the hallway so these stimuli do not grab his attention. Also, he should not be seated near other students' traffic patterns. Ideally, the child's desk should be at the front of a row so that other students and their distractions are out of his immediate visual field. He should also be seated close to where the teacher typically stands when presenting information. The teacher can then conveniently provide subtle gestures, move materials, and give an occasional physical prompt. It is also important to consider who is sitting next to the child. The child should be seated next to students who are typically on task and well organized, and who don't talk unnecessarily to classmates.

Microenvironment

Desk

The child's desk itself needs to be considered. The desk should be small enough so that the child's feet rest firmly on the floor. On the other hand, if it takes a shoehorn to squeeze the child into the desk, it is too small. Children who are in a desk that fits their body will, all things being equal, spend more time doing their schoolwork.

Daily Schedules

When students get off task, it is the teacher's job to get them back on task. Most children can be redirected back to task with a verbal directive. For example, the teacher might say, "Joan, you need to be doing your math." But a verbal directive often detonates an oppositional child.

A daily schedule works well with children who have oppositional and defiant behaviors because it visually reminds the children what they need to be doing. When these children are off task, they often look to the daily schedule for a self-generated redirection. If verbal cuing is needed, the teacher can ask a question rather than issue a directive. She might ask, "Justin, what does your schedule say?"

The daily schedule can use one of three levels of communication: objects, pic symbols, or written words.[2] To be useful, the schedule must correspond to the child's developmental level. A simple matching task will determine the correct communication system. If the child cannot readily match the communication symbols when doing a sorting task, then any communication system based on those symbols is not developmentally appropriate.

Object Schedules. Appropriate for preschoolers, an object schedule associates a unique object with each activity. For example, a 2-by-2-inch piece of carpet might be associated with "calendar time," the cardboard cylinder from a roll of toilet paper means "bathroom break," a crayon means "work at your desk," and a plastic spoon signals "lunch." Each of these objects is lined up on the daily-schedule shelf.

To understand how the system works, consider a student named Sam. The system is initiated as soon as Sam hangs up his coat in the morning. The teacher hands Sam a "check-schedule card," which is a 2-by-2-inch piece of posterboard with a black checkmark on it. Sam carries the check-schedule card to his daily-schedule shelf. There, he sees another check-schedule card on an envelope. This directs him to put his check-schedule card in the envelope. Immediately to his right, Sam sees a 2-by-2-inch piece of carpet and picks it up. Looking around the room, Sam sees an identical carpet square on the bottom of the wall. To "match" his carpet piece with the piece on the wall, he has to bend down almost to the floor. The matching is done more easily from the sitting position, so Sam sits down. And sitting on the floor is right where the teacher wants him. It's time for a calendar activity. When

Sam finishes calendar time, the teacher hands him another check-schedule card, which takes him back to the shelf holding his daily schedule. Since the carpet is gone, Sam sees the next salient visual stimulus: a crayon. It matches a crayon on his desk, and it means that he needs to go to his desk.

The daily schedule puts Sam in the right place doing the right thing without having to give him a single verbal directive. As anyone who has worked with oppositional children knows, a verbal directive can bring out these children's noncompliance and defiance.

Pic Symbols. Line drawings that represent the object are called pic symbols. Like an item from an object schedule, the pic symbol serves to constantly remind the child where he needs to go and what he will do when he gets there. Often, some strong stimulus distracts the child en route to his intended destination and he is drawn toward it. Maybe it is noise or the sight of another child playing with a block. But as with most stimuli, the intensity of the distracting stimulus fades, and the pic symbol in the child's hand reemerges as the dominant stimulus, serving to redirect him. All this happens without the teacher having to give a verbal directive. However, if a verbal prompt is needed, the pic symbol enables the teacher to ask a benign question. Rather than say, "Sam, sit down and do your math," the teacher can ask, "Sam, where do you need to be right now?" The pic symbol enables Sam to answer the question for himself.

🔑 *Key Concept*

When the teacher asks a child, "Where do you need to be right now?" the child should be able to look at his communication system and find the answer.

Occasionally, educators attempt to substitute photographs for either objects or pic symbols. The substitution seldom works because photographs contain too much detail and visual information.

Written Words. These represent the highest level in a visual communication system. A typical schedule taped on the side of a child's desk might look like this:

8:30   Pledge
8:35   Math
9:00   Reading
9:30   Bathroom Break
9:35   Social Studies
10:00 Recess

The schedule does not cover the entire day. If it did, the salient cues would merge into clutter. While the child is out during recess, the teacher replaces this half-morning schedule with a schedule for the rest of the morning's activities.

The schedule allows the teacher to get the student back on task without having to resort to a verbal directive. Consider the following exchange:

A Redirection

Justin finished his word-tracing worksheet before the rest of the students were done with theirs. Feeling bored, he looked around and spotted the fish tank. He walked over to investigate. While Justin was watching the fish, the rest of the students finished their worksheets. It was time for phonics, but Justin was still watching the fish.

"Justin, take your seat," Mrs. Smith said. "It's time for phonics." The directive sounded just enough like an order to visibly irritate Justin. Defiantly, he turned his back to Mrs. Smith and kept watching the fish.

Justin would have been more likely to get back to his desk if Mrs. Smith had asked, "Justin, what's on your schedule?" There is something objective, matter-of-fact, neutral about a question like that, and it is less likely to elicit defiance.

Work Structure

For students who are oppositional and also have attention problems, the materials in their desk often get them off task. The solution is to give the child an organizational system. In the most extreme case, it means removing everything from the child's desk.

Donald was a case in point. Everything in his desk was removed and put into "activity boxes"—shoeboxes labeled for each subject. There was an activity box for math, one for reading, and so on. Every morning, before the students arrived, Mr. Burke filled Donald's activity boxes with the materials needed for that day's lesson. The math box did not contain the entire math workbook. Instead, it contained only one worksheet and a sharpened pencil. When it was time for math, Mr. Burke put the math box on Donald's desk. Donald removed the materials and put the empty box on the floor. When he completed the work, Donald put it inside a "finished" box that sat beside his desk.

Donald's materials were organized along the lines of Structured Teaching. Although Structured Teaching was designed for organizing the work of children with autism, it is also useful for young children with oppositional and defiant behaviors or attention problems.[3] Structured Teaching is useful because it uses visual cues in lieu of verbal directives to provide the child with four essential questions: (1) What work needs to be done? (2) How much work needs to be done? (3) When is the work finished? and (4) What comes next?

1. *What work needs to be done?* This question is answered by the presence of three "workbaskets" placed on a shelf next to or near the child's desk. The workbaskets can be anything from cardboard boxes to plastic washtubs. On his desk, the child has four cards, each marked with either a color or a number, depending on the child's matching ability. Three of these cards match a color or a number on a particular workbasket. Working from left to right (which is always encouraged so that the child develops a useful habit), the child takes the first card and matches it to the first workbasket. He brings that workbasket to his desk and completes the tasks it contains. He continues in the same manner with the second and third cards and workbaskets.

2. *How much work needs to be done?* This question is answered by the tasks in the workbasket. When each task in the workbasket is completed, it goes into a "finished" basket.

3. *When is the work finished?* The work is finished when the child has completed everything in all three workbaskets.

4. *What comes next?* The fourth card answers this question. For children at a low developmental level, the fourth card is usually an object or a pic symbol associated with a short break or a fun activity. Even for older elementary children of normal ability, finishing work should lead to an opportunity to do an enjoyable activity.

Children at a higher developmental level may benefit from a box system, like the one used for Donald. As Donald learns to use the system, he can progress from having the teacher hand him a box to using his schedule system to prompt himself when it is time to get the box off the shelf and run his own work system.

Even middle school students with oppositional or attention problems can benefit from a work system. For them, colored notebooks or the colored tabs in a three-ring binder are useful. Each colored notebook or tab is associated with the materials from a particular class. An additional colored folder can hold uncompleted materials.

These children often benefit from a system that incorporates a homework assignment sheet like the one in Figure 3.2. On the form, the students write down the homework due in each class. The teacher initials it to confirm that the assignment is correct. The students initial the form when the work is completed. This form serves three purposes: (1) The teacher knows that the students have the correct assignment; (2) the students can review the form before leaving school to ensure that they have the necessary materials; and (3) other people have the necessary information to help monitor progress.

Tasks

Teachers can also apply environmental engineering to the tasks they ask the child to complete. The teacher needs to consider various aspects of the tasks, such as developmental level, visual clarity, a clear finish, and the presence of only one response set.

 *Key Concept*

In school, most of the child's noncompliance and defiance occurs because the presented task is too hard, lacks visual clarity, or has no clear finish.

Appropriate Developmental or Academic Level. Every activity presented to children with oppositional and defiant behaviors must be at their developmental or academic level. If oppositional children look at a task and cannot immediately see that they can do it, they almost certainly will react with negative behavior. To ensure that an assignment is appropriate, the teacher should have an updated list of

Figure 3.2
Homework Assignment Sheet

Name: _____

Date: _____

Subject	Homework to Do	Teacher	Student
Reading	Workbook: prob. 1–15, pg. 36		
Math	Odd # prob. on page 72		
Spelling			
Social Studies			
Language Arts			

the academic skills that the children have passed, the skills that are emerging, and the skills they cannot do. To ensure objectivity, this list might be prepared monthly, through diagnostic teaching, by a special educator and shared with the classroom teacher.

Visual Clarity. The tasks must have good visual clarity, meaning the child should be able to look at the task and know what needs to be done. A good way for a teacher to know if a task has sufficient visual clarity is to give the task, without any verbal instructions, to an adult who is not an educator. If the adult asks, "What do I do with this?" the task does not have sufficient visual clarity. If oppositional children look at a task and cannot immediately see what needs to be done, they will usually act out.

Clear Finish. The tasks need to have a clear finish. The child should be able to determine when the task is completed simply by looking at it. It is best to avoid tasks that do not have a clear finish. Of course, some tasks, like coloring, do not have a clear finish. In such cases, like coloring, the teacher may use a timer to signal the end of the activity. When the timer goes off, the task is "finished." However, many children do not respond well to a timer. For them, the task should either be avoided or be given more structure so that it has a clear finish. For example, Ryan, a 3-year-old with oppositional behaviors, had a three-step task to complete. He had to put a wooden stick into a film container, snap on the lid, and put the container in a box. In front of him was a box with three partitions. The first partition held five sticks, the second partition held five film containers, and the third partition was empty. The teacher's aide expected Ryan to put the film container in the third partition. When she presented the task to him, Ryan completed the first two steps. But after he snapped the lid on the container, he did not put the container in the third partition. Instead, after a brief hesitation, he threw it. The aide immediately gave him hand-on-hand assistance to get the other four containers into the third partition. However, before she presented the task to him again, she increased the structure of the task. A little box was securely taped upside down in the third partition. In the bottom of the box, which was now the top, were six holes, each just big enough to hold a film container. The hole farthest from Ryan's reach contained a finished film container. The entire top of the upside-down box was covered with a piece of red paper. By training, children using the Structured Teaching system learn that red means "completed." When the task was restructured so that it had more visual clarity, Ryan successfully completed it.

One Response Set. Each task should demand only one response set. Surprisingly, most workbooks, even those for the early grades, ask for two or more response sets on the same page. For example, in the top-left corner children are asked to circle the word that fits the sentence. In the bottom-right corner, they have to draw lines between words that rhyme. Many children have difficulty switching from one response set to another and usually need a directive from the teacher to initiate a shift in their response set. However, as mentioned before, when a teacher gives a directive to some children, they typically become noncompliant and defiant. To solve the problem of having more than one response set on a page, the teacher may cut the page in parts and use a copying machine to make a separate sheet for each part. Alternatively, everything on the page that is extraneous to the task may either be cut out or boldly crossed out with a black, felt-tipped pen.

 Key Concept

Question: How much environmental engineering is needed?
Answer: As much as it takes.

Assistance

Despite good environmental engineering or possibly even because of the demands that it puts on the teacher's time, it may be necessary to add staff. Some students even require a one-to-one aide. One of the aide's jobs is to make the teaching stimulus salient. If the child becomes distracted, the aide must quickly remove the distracting stimulus and refocus the child on the important one. If a presented task is beyond the child's ability, the aide must instantly modify it down to the child's level. For example, Jacob was given a math sheet with some math problems that involved regrouping and some that did not. He did not know how to regroup, and each time he came to a regrouping problem, he got angry. Seeing his anger, his aide quickly directed Jacob to a problem that did not involve regrouping and crossed out the remaining regrouping problems on the page. Similarly, if a task does not have good visual clarity, the aide needs to swiftly give the task more visual clarity. If the task lacks a clear finish, the aide needs to define the finish.

Specialists

Individualizing instruction is time-consuming and, depending on the child's needs, often requires specialized training. Increasingly, specialists are being used as a resource to the classroom teacher to enable more children to be mainstreamed as opposed to being "pulled out" of the classroom. Some children with conduct problems have learning needs and socialization needs that require the services of specialists.

Engineering Justin's Environment in Kindergarten

Seating Arrangement

At the end of the day on Friday, Mrs. Smith announced that when the students came back to school on Monday, they would find that their seat had been moved. Because Justin reveled in being the class clown and he had no problems understanding or following the teacher's instructions, his seat was moved to the back of the last row. From that position, it was no longer convenient for him to get other students' attention with his antics. It also gave Mrs. Johnson, his aide, a place to put her chair when she was working with him.

Daily Schedule

Justin received a written schedule. Because changes in the routine upset him, the teacher or the aide reviewed any change with him at the beginning of the day and explained the reason for it. Justin highlighted the change in yellow. When each activity was over, Justin crossed it off the list.

Initially, Mrs. Johnson read the schedule to Justin. Like most oppositional children, Justin interpreted her reading as "telling." "I can read!" he defiantly reminded her. "Yes, you can," Mrs. Johnson said, and she stopped reading the schedule to Justin. Similarly, when a redirection was necessary, Mrs. Smith did not say, "Justin, your schedule says that you should be doing your math." Instead, she asked, "Justin, what's next on your schedule?" Asking Justin a question gave him the feeling of being in control. Justin liked feeling in control.

Work Structure

Justin needed to have his work more structured, but he would have found workbaskets demeaning. Instead, Mrs. Smith put three plastic boxes on a nearby shelf. Each morning, she "loaded" the boxes with the appropriate activities, putting materials for each subject area activity in a separate box. When Justin went to the shelf, he worked from left to right at the various activities. When he completed a particular activity, he put it in a "finished" box—a red plastic tub. When Justin was at recess, Mrs. Smith or Mrs. Johnson reloaded his activity boxes.

In keeping with the concept that finishing work should earn play, Justin was allowed to read when he completed any assignment early. A book was always at his table. Mrs. Smith set his timer so that it rang at the end of the time allotted for that activity. When the bell rang, Justin put his book away, Mrs. Smith handed him a pencil, and he crossed that activity off his schedule.

Tasks

Justin did not need any downward adjustments of the tasks to fit his academic level. He also did not need any additional visual clarity. However, his tasks had to have a clear finish. If the task did not have a clear finish, Justin would do only a minimal amount of work and then claim he was ready to read his book.

Additional Assistance

Because Justin was often out of class as a result of his inability to control his behavior, the team agreed that a classroom aide was needed. Mrs. Johnson filled that role.

Engineering Cassandra's Environment in 3rd Grade

Seating Arrangement

When doing independent work, Cassandra made excessive demands on her teacher, Ms. Jones, for attention. Seating arrangements offered two possible solutions. One solution was to put Cassandra close to the teacher's desk, which is where Ms. Jones sat during the students' independent work time. The other solution was to put Cassandra as far as possible from the teacher's desk in the hope that she would demand attention less often if Ms. Jones were not readily accessible. Ms. Jones decided on the first alternative, not for Cassandra's sake, but for the other students. She anticipated that if Cassandra were diagonally across the room from her, she would disrupt too many students while she repeatedly went back and forth from her desk to the teacher's desk.

Daily Schedule

Despite her attention problems, Cassandra did not have difficulty moving from one academic task to the next, and she readily accommodated change. She had no need for a daily schedule.

Work Structure

During class instruction time, Cassandra did not need a work system. However, she did need a work system when working independently at her desk. Her work system consisted of a basket system, a "finished" box, and a reward of being able to play a computer game.

Tasks

Classroom observation revealed that Cassandra became oppositional when the teacher presented any assignment that involved reading, and sometimes she became oppositional during math instruction. Informal assessment and diagnostic teaching revealed that Cassandra's reading skills were about a year and a half below grade level. When reading, she relied almost exclusively on her sight vocabulary and made little use of phonetic decoding skills. When given tasks that required reading, she often became noncompliant and, when pushed, actively resisted doing the assignments.

Also, Cassandra was delayed in math. If she came to any problem beyond her ability when doing a math assignment, she stopped working altogether and glared at the teacher. When Ms. Jones came to help, Cassandra sulked and pouted rather than explain what kind of assistance she needed.

Thus, the tasks were a major problem for Cassandra. She needed tasks that were at her academic level, had good visual clarity and a clear finish, and demanded only one response set on each page. Ms. Jones changed Cassandra's assignments in three ways: (1) Cassandra left the classroom during reading time to receive one-to-one instruction at her ability level; (2) instead of giving Cassandra an entire math assignment, Ms. Jones gave her only four similar problems at a time; and (3) if language arts activities called for reading material and then responding by writing a sentence or two, Ms. Jones modified the activity so that Cassandra listened to the information being read and then selected between two possible answers.

Specialists

A retired teacher was hired to work one-to-one with Cassandra between 1:00 and 2:30 p.m. every day. She gave Cassandra her primary instruction in reading and provided support and guidance when Cassandra did math and language arts assignments.

Engineering Harry's Environment in 6th Grade

Seating Arrangement

In each of his departmentalized classes, Harry chose to sit in the back of the room. Therefore, to minimize the effects of his disruptive behavior, the teachers had to assign seats. In each class, they moved him to the middle of the classroom and surrounded him with several serious, on-task students who participated in class discussions. Even though Harry had problems paying attention and following the teacher's directions, he would not have accepted being moved to the front row, right next to the teacher.

Daily Schedule

In the middle school, a bell rang at the end of each class period. When the bell rang, Harry knew where to go. However, he was seldom ready to make the transition when the bell rang. By the time he reached a good finishing point, other students were coming into the room and disturbing his things. The commotion caused by the incoming wave of students made it even more difficult for Harry to gather his materials, and, in frustration, he often exploded. Making things even worse, Harry usually arrived at the next class late, disrupting the lesson as he slid by students to get to his desk.

To deal with these problems, it was necessary for Harry's teachers to foreshadow, or give some advance notice as the end of the class was approaching. Specifically, the teachers found it useful to announce, "Class is over in five minutes. Bring your work to a close," and, a few minutes later, "Class is over in three minutes. It's time to stop working and gather up your things."

Finally, Harry's schedule needed to be adjusted to better fit his predictable "states." Usually, Harry did not arrive at school fully awake. He was not ready at 8:30 in the morning to sit in an academic class and pay attention. He did much better in music, which involved more activity and body movement. A schedule with three consecutive academic classes also did not work. Harry could sit and listen for two classes in a row, at best. His best learning time was right after lunch, and so the class that made the most demands on his ability to pay attention was moved to that slot. Harry was failing history; in fact, his grade was so low that, according to the teacher, he had virtually no chance of getting a passing grade. Therefore, history was dropped, and Harry spent fourth period, just before lunch, in the resource room instead.

Work Structure

Harry had serious organizational problems. He was failing largely because he did not turn in finished assignments. The school counselor was asked to confer with Harry about this problem. Together they developed a plan. The counselor supplied Harry with a three-ring binder for his homework and arranged to have all his worksheets punched with three holes. His new schedule included an hour in the resource room at the end of the day. There, he received one-to-one assistance with any incomplete daily assignments. He arrived at the resource room each day with a task-completion sheet. Mr. Adams, the resource room teacher, kept the assignments that Harry completed, and he took responsibility for distributing them to the teachers. Harry left school each day with the incomplete assignments and appropriate materials.

Unlike most other students, Harry found it difficult to go to his locker each morning and get the materials needed for the next three hours of instruction. He was always arriving at class either without any materials or with the wrong materials. He was not ready for this level of responsibility, so a modification was made. Each teacher handed Harry the needed materials when he arrived at class. After class, Harry left the materials, such as the textbook, pencils, and workbooks, with the teacher. If he needed to take any materials home, those materials were put into the resource room teacher's mailbox.

Tasks

In addition to his problems with organization, below-grade-level skills were contributing to Harry's failure to complete homework. Diagnostic instruction determined that his math skills were three years below grade level and his reading comprehension was two years below grade level. He struggled with reading comprehension when a passage contained too many words outside of his reading vocabulary. As described below, a pocket calculator, special help, and adjustments in reading assignments addressed Harry's skill deficiencies.

Additional Assistance

Because Harry now spent two periods a day in the resource room, Mr. Adams, the resource room teacher, was available to provide additional assistance. He taught Harry how to use a pocket calculator, and Harry was allowed to use it in any class where it would be useful, particularly math. For all classes that required reading for information, he was pre-taught the key vocabulary words in all of the new material. This pre-teaching took place in the resource room. In addition, in classes that required considerable reading, his learning objectives were decreased in number and modified downward in difficulty.

4

Managing the Daily Antecedents

When discussing oppositional children, *antecedents* refers to events that occur just before a particular behavior is displayed. Not all antecedents that affect oppositional children can be environmentally engineered. Some decisive antecedents simply happen in the ebb and flow of the day. These daily antecedents can be divided into two categories: those that increase the likelihood of noncompliant, defiant behavior, and those that increase the likelihood of appropriate behavior. Obviously, the goal is to avoid the former and enhance the latter.

Antecedents to Avoid

Some antecedents predictably detonate oppositional children. Some examples include

- Hearing someone say "No!";
- Hearing a directive to stop doing something;
- Hearing a sharply worded directive to do something;
- Seeing any gesture, facial grimace, or body language that conveys disapproval; and
- Having idle time.

These antecedents to noncompliance and defiance must be avoided. Unfortunately, this is not easy to do. Educators who watch a child defiantly break a pencil are tempted to say, "That's enough of that," or, at a minimum, frown. When oppositional children detect the slightest signs of disapproval, they instantly become noncompliant and defiant.

Idle time by itself does not bring out oppositional and defiant behaviors. However, idle time tends to create opportunities for the child to get off task and then require some type of directive. Although the directive usually causes the child to become oppositional, idle time should be kept to a minimum.

Realistically, teachers are often not aware of a particular student's time on task. They simply have too many other things to attend to while instructing and guiding the learning of some 25 students. It can be useful to have an observer record the target child's time on task. Typically, observations of easily distracted children show that they do not use independent work time productively and that most of their oppositional behaviors occur at this time.

Unique Antecedents

For some children, the antecedents that trigger noncompliance are unique. For example, Rusty, a 2nd-grade student, transferred to a new school in late November. He wasted no time acquainting his teacher, Mr. Allen, with one of his antecedents for noncompliance.

Rusty Doesn't Salute Anything

At the beginning of the school day, Mr. Allen asked the students to stand for the pledge of allegiance to the flag. Rusty remained seated. Thinking that Rusty had not heard him, Mr. Allen walked over and said, "Rusty, please stand up for the pledge."

Rusty shook his head, "No."

Mr. Allen said, "Rusty, we always stand for the pledge." Sneering defiantly, Rusty threw his book on the floor and firmly planted his head on his desk. Rusty made it clear that he wasn't going to stand for the pledge. Wisely, Mr. Allen withdrew. Rusty won the first round.

Mr. Allen immediately realized that for Rusty the directive to stand for the pledge was an antecedent for noncompliance. He decided that Rusty would go to the resource room first thing in the morning. There, he would spend 15 minutes studying his spelling words or doing math problems on a computer. By then, the directive to stand for the pledge and the other directives associated with the ritual of getting the class under way would have passed, and Rusty could return to his classroom.

For Kenny, the antecedent for defiance was a directive from his teacher, Ms. Morrison, to get back on task. Ms. Morrison reported that most of Kenny's noncompliance occurred during cooperative-learning activities. However, eliminating cooperative-learning activities was not an option. Ms. Morrison valued them. Classroom observation revealed that the antecedent to Kenny's off-task behavior was the passage of a certain amount of time. Kenny could sustain his attention on a task for about four minutes, but not much longer. The solution was a timer. Ms. Morrison set the timer for four minutes. When the timer rang, Kenny sought out Ms. Morrison and reported what his cooperative-learning group was doing. Ms. Morrison used that opportunity to focus Kenny's attention on the next stage of the project. She reset the timer and Kenny worked for another four minutes. This provided a total of eight minutes of cooperative learning, which was long enough for the 1st-grade cooperative-learning tasks.

For Cassandra, a 3rd-grade student, the antecedent for passive-aggressive sulking was waiting time. Classroom observation revealed that when Cassandra raised her hand to ask for teacher assistance, she would wait quietly for about 10 seconds. If the teacher, Ms. Jones, had not come to help by then, Cassandra would repeatedly interrupt Ms. Jones as she attempted to work with other students. The solution was to give Cassandra a green card. When she had a question, Cassandra got out of her desk and gave the green card to the teacher. She then returned to her desk and watched the minute hand on the big clock at the front of the room. She was expected to sit quietly for one minute. Another remedy for Cassandra's situation involved making sure the work was tailored to her skill level. When her work was adjusted as necessary, she was capable of doing most of her desk work without additional assistance.

Praise as an Antecedent for Noncompliance and Defiance

Some antecedents for noncompliance are counterintuitive. Consider the following scenario:

A Strange Antecedent for Defiance

Brandon had been sitting at his desk for 10 minutes working diligently on his printing worksheet. Mrs. Thompson, always vigilant for opportunities to praise her students, walked up to him. Putting her hand lightly on his shoulder, she bent down and said, "Brandon, that is really good printing." Angrily, Brandon broke his pencil in half and tore up the worksheet.

In this case, praise was an antecedent for an outburst. When oppositional children are praised, they often react negatively. Some people speculate that oppositional children react defiantly when praised because accepting praise is the harbinger of being controlled. Praise has meaning only if the person receiving it values the person dispensing it. However, valuing implies listening, and listening connotes control. Even 3-year-old children understand this dynamic. So at the first hint of praise, oppositional children often become defiant and even aggressive.

Teaching oppositional children to accept praise must be done slowly and carefully. The prerequisite is trust. The educator must ensure the child that he is emotionally and physically safe in the teacher's presence. In particular, the child must become convinced that the educator will not punish him. This does not mean that the educator approves of everything the child does. It also does not mean that the teacher never intervenes when the child displays unacceptable behavior. It means that regardless of the child's behavior, the educator always keeps control of his or her emotions. Any intervention to control the child's behavior is done in a calm, predictable manner that protects the child's dignity.

Key Concept

Trust is the foundation for building a relationship with an oppositional child, and trust is never given. It has to be earned.

Left to develop at its own rate, trust will evolve slowly. But teachers can do various things to expedite the development of trust. A good trust-building activity is spending time with the child doing something the child enjoys. If it is a rainy day and the children cannot go out for recess, the teacher might join the child in putting together a puzzle, constructing with building blocks, shooting baskets in the gym, or catching a ball. Whatever activity is chosen, it must be the child's activity, not the teacher's. For example, no trust will be built if the teacher says to the oppositional girl, "Let me show you how to play a new song on the piano." The purpose of the activity is to bring the teacher into the child's world, not to usher the child into the adult's world. Also, the selected activity must not have a clear winner and loser, a "faster" and a "slower," or a "better" and a "worse."

 Key Concept

Participating with the child in a high-interest activity can help establish trust.

Because the activity is a vehicle around which to build a relationship, the educator must be careful not to become directive. If the child is putting a roof on a block structure but the construction technique is faulty, the teacher should not point out the error. Rather the teacher should help the child place the blocks in accordance with the child's design and then act surprised when the structure collapses. In other words, the child not only chooses the activity, the child chooses the process, and whatever process is chosen is acceptable.

Even when the educator skillfully enters the child's world to engage in a participatory activity, it is not easy to gain the student's trust. As soon as the child begins to think that he might be emotionally and physically safe in the teacher's presence, he will decide to test that possibility. He will intentionally escalate his noncompliance, defiance, or aggression to a new level. In the face of unprecedented levels of defiance, some educators erroneously conclude that their efforts have been to no avail. In frustration, they lose control of their emotions and intentionally or possibly inadvertently punish the child. If that happens, the child concludes that he can't trust the teacher.

An observer with a practiced eye can tell when children are "testing" the teacher. In cases involving aggression, the child is testing if the aggression lacks its usual impulsiveness. In cases involving noncompliance, the child is testing if there is no plausible antecedent. In cases involving defiance, the child is testing if the defiance is out of proportion to the perceived insult. In addition, the child is testing if he makes sure the educator sees the behavior; and the child is almost certainly testing if, after committing the act, he looks at the educator to catch his or her reaction. Knowing this dynamic, educators can learn to control their reactions.

Getting Brandon to Accept Praise

Brandon, a kindergarten student, was learning to write various letters. Walking by his desk, Mrs. Thomson commented, "Brandon is printing a B." She purposely used third-person language and labeled a specific behavior. Third-person language does not imply as close a bond as second-person language. At this early stage and lacking trust, Brandon would not have accepted second-person language. Even hearing third-person language caused Brandon to momentarily stop printing.

A few days later, Brandon's body language indicated that he now accepted Mrs. Thompson's third-person labeling. He no longer paused, flexed a muscle, or subtly pulled away from Mrs. Thompson when she praised him. So she switched to second-person labeling. "Brandon," she said, "you solved the 3 + 4 problem." This time, he showed signs of agitation. The muscle flexed in his forearm and his jaw tightened. But she moved on, and Brandon went back to his math worksheet.

The next step was to praise his work, but using third-person language. "Brandon's printing is very neat," Mrs. Thompson commented, walking by his desk. When Brandon's nonverbal behavior suggested that he was accepting being praised in the third person, Mrs. Thompson said, "Brandon, you printed that B very neatly. I like it."

 Key Concept

Teaching students who are particularly oppositional and defiant to accept praise is usually a slow process.

The process of teaching the child to accept praise is slow, gradual, and interspersed with occasional regressions. The key steps are to begin with third-person labeling, label "on the fly," and slowly move toward second-person praising based on subtle readings of the child's nonverbal indications of either irritation or acceptance. It is also important to avoid eye contact because eye contact implies that an acknowledgment is expected.

Dealing with the Unknown Antecedents

Some antecedents for noncompliance and defiance are unknown to teachers, but their effects are observable. Most teachers quickly learn to spot when children come to school in the morning primed to explode. Each child emits unique warning signs. A particular child might come in and give the teacher a "don't-even-think-about-it" glare. Another child might come in with her head down and slump into her desk or go into a corner, attempting to shut out the world. Yet another child might be "bouncing off the walls." Whatever the cues, the child is saying, "I'm having a tough day. Cut me some slack." That is exactly what the teacher should do. What the child needs at the moment varies widely from individual to individual. Some children can center themselves if they are just allowed to sit at their desk without having any demands placed on them for a while. Other children can get themselves out of a bad mood by doing a favorite activity or an academic task slightly below their ability level. A few children need to leave the room and go to a supportive place, such as the resource room, the counselor's office, or even the gym, where they can calm themselves.

Antecedents to Enhance

Choices

Oppositional children like choices because choices give them a sense of control. It is advisable to give children choices even when the request is benign: "Tony, would you like to color those ducks brown or would you like to color them yellow?" Choices are often useful when attempting to redirect the child away from an unacceptable behavior. Consider the following situation.

The Spitball Thrower

Mr. Nelson saw Sam, a 5th grader, making spitballs. As Mr. Nelson watched, Sam got ready to throw a spitball across the room. "Sam," he said, "Don't you dare throw that!" Everyone in the room turned and looked at Sam, his arm poised to launch the missile. "Don't throw it," Mr. Nelson repeated. Sam threw it.

For Sam, the directive not to throw the spitball put him in a lose-lose situation. If he threw the spitball, he would be asking for whatever consequence Mr. Nelson was going to administer. But if Sam didn't throw it, he'd be backing down from the teacher in front of his peers.

Instead of issuing an implied ultimatum, Mr. Nelson could have ignored the portending behavior and redirected Sam with a choice between two acceptable behaviors. "Sam," he could have said, "would you like to pass out these papers or do you want to finish your math worksheet?" Mr. Nelson also could have asked a private question instead of issuing a public command. Instead of saying, "Sam, don't you dare throw that!" Mr. Nelson could have walked over to Sam's desk and quietly asked, "Sam, are you making a good decision right now?" When intervening to disrupt a problematic behavior, private communications work better than public ones, and questions work better than commands.

Foreshadowing

For most schoolchildren, the end of one activity and the beginning of another comes as no surprise. The typical 1st grader understands that math must be coming because letter sounds is wrapping up, and math comes right after letter sounds. She also knows it must be math time because her stomach is growling, and math comes right before lunch. She knows it must be math time because the little hand on the clock is on the number nearly to the top and the big hand is pointing straight down. She notices that Fred has taken out his math book, and Fred always knows what is coming next. So when the teacher says, "Finish up your phonics and get out your math," the child is ready.

But children who have attention problems do not read these environmental cues. They are too busy responding to the extraneous stimuli impinging upon them. When the change in schedule comes, they are not ready for it. For example, an oppositional child has four items left on a phonics paper when the teacher says, "Students, get out your math workbook." But, wanting to finish his phonics, the child ignores the teacher and keeps working. Meanwhile, the other students have taken out their math books, and the teacher is starting to explain the lesson. Then she notices that Joe, the oppositional child, is still doing his phonics lesson. To get his attention, the teacher asks Joe a question about the math lesson. Angrily, Joe rips up his phonics paper and throws it on the floor.

Many oppositional children need to have upcoming changes in activities foreshadowed. A timer is a useful device for foreshadowing change and signaling the end of the activity. For example, when three minutes remain for art, the teacher sets a timer and says, "Three minutes left to color." When it is down to one minute, the teacher announces, "One minute left to color." When the timer rings, the teacher says, "Art time is over."

🔑 *Key Concept*

Most antecedents that promote positive behavior in oppositional children work because they cue behavior change at that moment without giving a verbal directive.

Completing a set number of problems is useful to foreshadow change for children who are at a lower developmental level. For example, if the child is working on a math worksheet, the teacher might circle three problems and say, "Finish these three problems and then it will be time to put away the math worksheet." Similarly, if the child is playing during recess, the teacher might say, "Shoot three more baskets, and then recess will be over."

A Caveat

Managing daily antecedents is something of an art form. Like art, it is an activity for which some people have an innate gift and others have no apparent talent. However, most people are somewhere between the two extremes. They understand that daily antecedents affect the children's behavior, but they can identify specific antecedents for particular children only in retrospect. However, these educators are on the learning curve. With time, practice, and reflection, they will be able to identify each child's unique indicators of a pending explosion and effectively prevent the eruption. When educators get to this level, they may be called master teachers.

The checklist in Figure 4.1 provides a way to help educators manage the daily antecedents. It includes space for recording progress in getting a child to accept praise.

Figure 4.1
Checklist for Managing the Daily Antecedents

Antecedents to Avoid

❏ Saying "No" or "Don't"
❏ Directives to stop doing a particular behavior
❏ Sharply worded directives to do a particular behavior
❏ Gestures, facial grimace, or body language that conveys disapproval
❏ Idle time for the student

Presence of Unique Antecedents

❏ Have the antecedents been identified?
❏ Is there a need for a classroom observation to do a functional behavior analysis?
❏ Is there a plan to avoid or at least mitigate those antecedents?

Antecedents to Increase

❏ Choices
❏ Foreshadowing

Teaching the Child to Accept Praise

❏ Third-person labeling
  Date initiated _____
  Date accepted _____

❏ Labeling on the fly

❏ Second-person labeling
  Date initiated _____
  Date accepted _____

❏ Third-person praise
  Date initiated _____
  Date accepted _____

❏ Second-person praise
  Date initiated _____
  Date accepted _____

Managing Justin's Daily Antecedents

Antecedents to Avoid

Justin predictably was noncompliant and defiant if he was given a verbal directive. So keeping verbal directives to a minimum was essential. However, when the teacher gave a verbal directive to the entire class, Justin would look around to see how the other students responded. If they acted on the directive, Justin would follow their lead and comply. He probably was not complying to please the teacher; rather, he complied because he liked to be a leader, and it was hard for him to lead if the entire class was marching off in a different direction.

Justin was ambivalent about praise. He did not react to praise with defiance or noncompliance. Yet praise did not enhance his behavior. Frankly, Justin did not value his teacher, Mrs. Smith, and until he did, her praise had no meaning for him.

Antecedents to Enhance

Justin responded well to choices. They met his need to be in control. So Mrs. Smith gave Justin choices between acceptable alternatives in lieu of using verbal directives. If it was severely cold outside, and knowing that Justin was apt to refuse to go out for recess, Mrs. Smith would ask, "Justin, do you want to go to recess or do you want to go the library and read your book?" If Justin was out of his seat when he should be doing his math assignment, Mrs. Smith asked, "Justin, do you want to work on math in the study carrel or in the resource room with Mrs. Johnson?"

Asking Justin questions that caused him to evaluate his behavior also worked. For example, if Justin was still reading his dinosaur book when the math lesson started, it did not work for Mrs. Smith to say, "Justin, put away your book now." Rather, he responded better if Mrs. Smith asked, "Justin, what should you be doing right now?"

For Justin, changes in the schedule needed to be foreshadowed. Not only did he have difficulty with change per se, but he became defiant and oppositional when he failed to make the transition and had to be given a directive. A timer provided an effective way to foreshadow change for Justin. As she set the timer, Justin's aide would say, "Math is over in five minutes. When the bell rings, be ready to put your math paper away."

Managing Cassandra's Daily Antecedents

Antecedents to Avoid

In consultation with Cassandra's teacher, Ms. Jones, the school psychologist did a series of short classroom observations and recorded antecedent-behavior-consequence (ABC) information about Cassandra's daily incidents of noncompliance. The data showed that the antecedent for most of Cassandra's oppositional behavior was the teacher saying "Stop that!" or issuing some type of reprimand when Cassandra did something that was inappropriate but that portended no harm to anyone or anything. For example, Cassandra might be organizing the contents of her desk when she was supposed to be studying spelling words.

When Ms. Jones saw the data, she began to ignore Cassandra's inappropriate behaviors that did not affect others and used redirection techniques on the remaining inappropriate behaviors. As a result, Cassandra's incidents of noncompliance dropped 75 percent.

Ms. Jones valued her one-on-one time with students. She liked them to come up to her desk so that she could work individually with each of them. However, while she was working intently and productively with a student, many of the other children were either waiting to get her attention or quietly talking with each other. In short, during Ms. Jones's one-on-one instruction time, the rest of the students were often not working. Fortunately, most of the students could satisfactorily manage this unstructured time without disrupting the classroom, but not Cassandra. She persistently interrupted Ms. Jones in an attempt to vie for the teacher's attention. If she could not adequately command Ms. Jones's attention, Cassandra stopped all work and sat at her desk with her arms folded across her chest and glared at Ms. Jones. When Ms. Jones came to help, Cassandra would not accept any assistance. She just pouted.

Three solutions helped address the problem. First, Ms. Jones increased the amount of direct instruction with class participation and therefore decreased the amount of time students spent working independently. Second, when the students were working independently, Cassandra used a schedule to work on tasks that were at her ability level and that had good visual structure and a clear finish. When she completed each task, she crossed it off her schedule. When her schedule was completed, she could play a game on the computer in the back of the room. Third, Ms. Jones gave Cassandra a timer to use during independent work time. After three minutes, when all the sand had run through the glass, she could go to Ms. Jones's desk and ask a question or have her work verified.

Cassandra also had behavior problems on the bus, and idle time was her nemesis. It was decided that the bus driver would privately visit with Cassandra to discuss the kinds of things that Cassandra was doing on the bus that distracted him so much that everyone's safety was threatened. The bus driver suggested a possible solution. He would hand Cassandra a portable radio with a headset when she got on the bus. She could listen to the radio all the way home. When she got off the bus, Cassandra would give the radio back to the bus driver.

Cassandra had no detectable unusual antecedents for oppositional behavior. Also, she did not become defiant when praised. She loved it.

Managing Harry's Daily Antecedents

Antecedents to Avoid

Harry became livid whenever a teacher gave a nonverbal sign that communicated disapproval, but many of his teachers flashed these signs of disapproval unconsciously. It was necessary to train them to be aware of how they conveyed their disapproval to Harry. The teachers were put into pairs, and each member of the team was asked to observe the other member during a class period and to give feedback. The teachers learned that they did more things to indicate disapproval than they were aware of. For example, they sighed, rolled their eyes, drummed their fingers, or looked away. With this increased awareness, the teachers markedly reduced their messages of disapproval, and Harry caused fewer classroom disruptions.

In addition, Harry often became defiant and disruptive when he was given a directive to do something. For example, when a teacher told Harry to get out his worksheet, Harry would get out the worksheet but not work on it. Instead, he would wait until the teacher wasn't looking at him, and he would make silly noises, whisper obscene one-liners to his nearby classmates, or "accidentally" drop a book off his desk so that it hit the floor with a loud bang.

Some days, Harry came to school in a bad mood. He could also get into one of these moods during unsupervised times, such as when students were in the hall between classes, or during lunch. When Harry was in one of his moods, he went to any and every length to disrupt the class. Typically, the teacher ordered Harry out of the classroom and sent him to the principal's office, where he got after-school detention. Being ordered out of the class counted as an unexcused absence if Harry missed more than 20 minutes of the class. According to school policy, 15 unexcused absences resulted in failing the class. Harry was on the verge of failing some classes simply because of too many unexcused absences.

The solution was for Harry to go to see Mr. Adams in the resource room first thing in the morning. Mr. Adams reviewed with Harry his preparations for the day, and he also helped Harry center his thoughts on school. A system was developed for Harry to leave a classroom and go to the resource room if he evidenced incipient disruptive behaviors in class. The teachers agreed that if Harry left the class at a subtle prompt from the teacher and took his work with him, he would not be given an unexcused absence.

Antecedents to Enhance

Harry responded well to choices. Choices appealed to his sense of being in control, and they worked effectively to redirect him away from inappropriate activities. For example, when Harry started to make "armpit noises," the teacher would say, "Harry, would you like to distribute tomorrow's homework assignments to the class, or do you want to continue working on your assignment?"

He particularly needed foreshadowing to signal that the class was coming to an end. It worked best if the teacher gave the foreshadowing to the entire class. So the teacher might call out, "There are five minutes left. Start wrapping up your work," and later, "There is one minute left. It's time to start putting things away."

5

Removing the Child from the Classroom

Oppositional children occasionally need to be removed from the classroom. This is necessary when they display behavior that could hurt people, damage property, or seriously disrupt the teaching and learning environment. Unfortunately, under these conditions the child's removal from the classroom usually occurs in a manner that escalates defiance and aggression. However, with careful planning the child can be removed with little or no resistance and with minimal disruption to the class.

☞ *Key Concept*

The child is removed only to protect people and property and to ensure a viable teaching and learning environment.

To create an environment that enables removal with minimal disruption, it is first necessary to accept that children who were born with difficult temperaments are not capable of the same levels of polite, thoughtful behavior as other students. For example, despite a classroom rule to raise a hand before talking, children who are impulsive are going to blurt out their thoughts. Despite a classroom rule to be seated while the teacher is presenting a lesson, such children are apt to get up to sharpen their pencils. If violating rules has consequences, the teacher will daily, if not hourly, be punishing the impulsive child.

Only one solution is possible. Some classroom rules—those designed to promote social skills—have to be waived for oppositional, defiant, or impulsive children. The rules should be replaced with others that reflect the teacher's need to protect people from getting hurt, to prevent the destruction of property, and to keep the learning environment functional. These concepts need to be stated in terms the child can understand, and they should not number more than four.

The child must participate in developing these rules. The process is simple. An educator, usually the school psychologist, the counselor, or the principal, simply asks the child, "What kinds of things cannot be permitted in the classroom?" Surprisingly, in many cases the child will have a much longer and more stringent list than the educators. This is a good beginning. It gives the educator an opportunity to show the child that he or she is actually reasonable—a concept these students find hard to believe. From that auspicious beginning, the educator provides the guidance and support to enable the child to identify the behaviors that cannot be permitted in the classroom. For example, with guidance Justin stated that he could not do the following:

- Hit, kick, or push people.
- Throw things.
- Tip over desks.

🔑 *Key Concept*

The child helps to develop the list of behaviors that necessitate removal from the classroom.

When asked, Justin was able to explain why he should not do these things. He realized that it was not acceptable to hurt people, to take things that weren't his, or to break things. Like most oppositional children, when Justin hit, kicked, or threw things, it was not a single incident. He was out of control. If he remained in the classroom, his aggression would escalate. He needed to leave the classroom. When he discussed these issues with a supportive, nonpunishing educator, Justin was able to understand this necessity.

A System for Voluntarily Leaving the Room

Laying the Groundwork

In a process borrowed from Reality Therapy, the child is asked what should happen if he engages in any inappropriate and unacceptable behaviors.[1] In Justin's case, the school psychologist working with him asked what should happen if he did things that might hurt people or break things. Initially, Justin did not give a good answer. He thought his teacher, Mrs. Smith, could leave him alone. But with the psychologist's support, he examined this solution and came to realize Mrs. Smith could not leave him alone if he was about to hit another student. Gradually, Justin came to understand that if he was about to hurt someone or break property, he needed to leave the classroom.

The school psychologist told Justin that he was not being punished by leaving the classroom, and that he was not leaving the classroom to be punished. He was leaving the classroom so that no one got hurt and nothing got broken. He would go to a quiet place where he could regain control. When he was calm, he could return to the classroom.

The psychologist asked Justin what activity he would like to do when he was out of the classroom. Justin wanted to work on a puzzle. So he and his aide, Mrs. Johnson, selected a puzzle, and they put it in the "calming room." The psychologist showed Justin a piece of the puzzle and told him that when he seemed to be getting upset and he might hurt someone or break property, Mrs. Johnson would hand him the puzzle piece, and she would go with him to the calming room. There, Justin could work on the puzzle until he felt sufficiently calm to return to the classroom. If necessary and with Justin's concurrence, the aide sometimes would bring academic tasks for him to work on in the calming room.

The importance of laying this groundwork cannot be overstated. Without the groundwork, the child sees the teacher-imposed necessity to leave the classroom as another situation in which an adult is trying to take away his control. If the child has this perspective, there is no way he is going to submit and he becomes defiant. The entire situation acquires a lose-lose dynamic. Either the child submits and loses his sense of control, or he resists, and physical confrontation develops. Laying the groundwork changes the dynamic. It is the child's plan. No one is trying to control him. The educator is working with him to help him fulfill his plan. Leaving the classroom now takes on a win-win dynamic.

Developing Justin's Plan

"Justin," the school psychologist said, "thank you for taking the time to visit with me. I phoned your mother, and she said it was okay if you are a little late getting home. But I want to know if that is okay with you, too."

"Sure," Justin said hesitantly.

"Justin, the principal told me that you have been sent down to her office almost every day this week. She is concerned that you are missing so much class time, and she wanted me to talk with you. The principal thought maybe you and I could come up with a solution. But how do you feel about being sent to the principal's office? Do you see that as a good thing or a bad thing?"

"Oh, it's probably a bad thing. It sure makes my mom mad when she finds out," Justin replied.

"Okay. I hear you saying that it is a bad thing to get sent to the principal's office. Would you like some help figuring out what to do so that you do not get sent to the principal's office?"

"I guess so," Justin said.

"Good. We'll see what we can figure out. Maybe the first place to start is figuring out why Mrs. Smith asks you to leave the room. Why do you do think Mrs. Smith asks you to leave the room and go the principal's office?" the school psychologist asked.

"I think she gets mad. When the teacher gets mad, she sends me down to the office," Justin conjectured.

"Are there any things that you do that cause her to get mad?" the school psychologist asked.

"No," Justin said emphatically. His response was typical. Most elementary children do not recognize the behaviors that cause them to be removed from the classroom. In their eyes, the teacher simply "gets mad" and then the child is out of the room. Their position holds a grain of truth. Most teachers do their best to tolerate and ignore behavior as long as they can and give a series of redirections and even warnings before they remove the child from the room. However, the child misinterprets the teacher's attempt to give him a chance. After all, throwing a book 10 minutes ago was overlooked, but throwing a piece of paper now got him removed. Obviously, throwing did not cause the removal. In the child's eyes, he was removed when the teacher "got mad."

"Justin," the school psychologist said, "if you were the teacher, when would you decide that a child needs to be removed from class? What rules would you have?"

"I'm never gonna be a teacher," Justin countered.

"Well, as a student in the room, when do you think a child should be removed? Or let me put it another way: What might a child do that means he needs to leave the room?"

"They have to listen to the teacher," Justin replied.

"Give me an example," the school psychologist said.

"Today the teacher told Joe to get out his pencil, and he didn't. He should have," Justin said.

"What happened then?" the school psychologist asked.

"The rest of us did our printing, but not Joe. He was playing with a rubber band," Justin explained.

"Did playing with a rubber band hurt anyone?" the school psychologist asked. "Did it stop you from getting out your pencil and doing your printing?"

"No," Justin said, seeing the point.

"Justin, what if a student hits someone? Should he have to leave the room?"

"Yes!" Justin replied. "He should leave."

"I think so, too, Justin. Why do we think a student who hits another person should have to leave the room?" the school psychologist asked.

"Because no one would come to school if they were going to be hit,"
Justin replied.

"Right. No one would come to school if they were going to be hit.
That student should be removed so he cannot hit anyone. What other
thing might a student do that means he should be removed from the class?"

With minimal guidance, Justin completed the list of rules for when a
child should be removed from the classroom.

Building a Relationship

In Justin's case, everyone involved believed he did not like Mrs.
Johnson, the classroom aide. For her part, Mrs. Johnson was understandably afraid of Justin. Clearly, any plan that Justin developed would
not work unless he and Mrs. Johnson strengthened their relationship.

 Key Concept

*The educator who is designated to facilitate the implementation of the
plan must have a good relationship with the child.*

Mrs. Johnson came to the clinic immediately after morning
kindergarten. In the clinic, she and Justin "played." Using a modest
amount of structure, they did various things together. They worked on
puzzles, shot baskets (Justin did most of the shooting), ate lunch, and,
alternating page by page, read out loud to each other a book about
dinosaurs, Justin's favorite topic. During this activity, Mrs. Johnson
skillfully got Justin to share with her a lot of information that he
knew about various types of dinosaurs. Justin's face beamed when he
told Mrs. Johnson such things as what the environment was like
where the sauropod lived. It was clear by the fourth day that Justin
and Mrs. Johnson had formed the relationship needed to support the

implementation of Justin's plan. That day, when they accidentally met at the front door and walked together to the clinic rooms, Justin reached out and took Mrs. Johnson's hand.

Getting Commitment

The school psychologist congratulated Justin for having developed a good plan for protecting people from getting hurt and preventing property from being broken. The plan was typed up as if it were a legal document (see Figure 5.1). The school psychologist, Mrs. Smith, Mrs. Johnson, and Justin duly signed the plan. It was called Justin's Plan, and indeed it was his plan.

 Key Concept

The child helps to develop the plan to leave the classroom. It is "the child's" plan.

The psychologist asked Justin to share his plan with others. With the necessary preplanning to ensure a proper reception, Justin shared his plan with the school counselor and then the principal. At Justin's suggestion, he even shared the plan with his mother. After Justin had shared his plan three times, he knew it well. In addition, important people had praised him for making such a good plan, and he had made a public commitment to follow it.

Preparation

Unless the people involved take additional steps, the oppositional child will, in the heat of a crisis, forget the plan. It is necessary to go through several role-plays in which the offense—appearing to be on the verge of hurting someone or breaking property—is committed, and the hero—the oppositional child—decides to calmly leave the scene. In Justin's case, the first role-play was with the school psychologist. Justin pretended that he was about to hit a classmate. Without

Figure 5.1
Justin's Plan

Why I might need to leave the room:

Sometimes I need to leave the room so that everyone is safe, no one gets hurt, and nothing gets broken. I need to leave if I am about to

- Hit someone,
- Kick someone,
- Throw something, or
- Break something.

My plan to leave the room:

When I get upset and might do something that could hurt someone or break something, I will leave the room and go with Mrs. Johnson (the aide) to work on my puzzle. We will go to the small room in the back of the library. When I feel calm, I can return to the classroom.

If I feel myself getting upset, I can ask Mrs. Johnson for the puzzle piece. She will hand me the puzzle piece, and I can leave the classroom and go the library.

If Mrs. Johnson feels that I am getting upset, she can hand me the puzzle piece. Anytime Mrs. Johnson hands me the puzzle piece, I will leave the room and go work on my puzzle.

No need to go home:

Anytime I leave the room to go work on my puzzle, neither my mother nor my dad will be called, and I will not have to go home. Instead, I can come back to the room when I am calm.

Justin	Jon Williams, School Psychologist

Mrs. Smith, Teacher	Mrs. Johnson, Aide

saying a word, the school psychologist handed Justin the puzzle piece and subtly gestured for him to leave the room. Justin repeated the role-play with his teacher, and then with his aide. Next, the role-play was moved to Justin's empty classroom. Finally, the aide and Justin privately went through two role-plays of the plan when other students were in the room.

It may not be necessary for a particular child to leave the room. Perhaps the child can become calm simply by going to the back of the room and sitting at a study carrel. In time, Justin reached this point. If he was on the verge of losing control or had actually lost control, he was able to go behind a partition in the back of the room and read a book until he was calm. Sometimes Justin became so engrossed in his book that he'd keep reading long after he was calm enough to return to the classroom. The teacher devised a simple solution. Because it usually took Justin about five minutes to calm himself, the reading material she put in the calming area was a magazine article that took only about five minutes to read.

A few children reach a point at which they can calm themselves by simply putting their head on their desk for three minutes. However, this is rare. The point is that it is not essential that the child leave the classroom. If the child can become calm and remain in the classroom, so much the better.

In theory, the intervention occurs before the child actually hurts someone or destroys property. However, the plan does not always proceed as written. Occasionally, the child's outburst is so instantaneous that someone gets hurt or something gets broken before the intervention can be made. That is unfortunate. However, such an "accident" does not mean that the child needs to be briskly removed from the classroom and sent to the principal for punishment. Instead, the situation, now more than ever, calls for skillful implementation of the plan.

Teachable Moments

Three teachable moments are associated with the implementation of the plan. The first teachable moment occurs the three to four times that the child follows the plan. After each success, the educator should enthusiastically praise the child for this ability to follow the plan.

The second teachable moment comes after following the plan becomes routine. Then the educator helps the child reflect on the behavior that necessitated his removal from the classroom. It is important that the child understand that the teacher did not have him removed for no reason. Rather, he was removed because his behavior threatened to hurt someone or to damage property, or it interfered with the teaching and learning process. In other words, the child needs to be able to identify the behavior that necessitated the removal from the classroom, and he needs to take responsibility for it.

The third teachable moment comes when the child readily recognizes his responsibility for the behavior. Then the educator helps the child think about what he could have done in the situation to avoid the behavior that necessitated the removal. This needs to be a discussion, not a "telling." Again, the child is responsible for developing a plan for avoiding the behavior that necessitated the removal. Most children will want to develop a "stop" plan; for example, "When I am about to tear up my papers, I will stop." Stop plans seldom work. "Instead" plans are more apt to work: "When I get angry, instead of tearing up the paper I will take three deep breaths." Or "Instead of tearing up the paper, I will take my pencil and scribble big black marks along the edge." Finally, before the child returns to the classroom, he should review the rules for staying in the classroom.

Training the Educators

In the moment of crisis, whether the plan gets successfully implemented depends a great deal on the skills of the educator. The educator's first task is to ignore any carnage and calmly begin the facilitation. If the educator becomes tense, the child will perceive it and respond in kind. Second, the educator must not use any body language, gestures, or words that connote disapproval. At this moment, the child expects punishment and disapproval. If he detects that it is coming, he will not implement the plan. For example, the aide should not say, "Justin! Don't you dare throw that! You need to work on your puzzle." Even if the aide uses such benign language as "Justin, you are getting out of control. Let's go work on the puzzle," she is connoting disapproval. The *best* language is *no* language. The aide should simply hand Justin the puzzle piece. If Justin does not adopt a slightly softer demeanor, indicating that he is moving toward implementing the plan, the aide might need to ask Justin, "What should you do with the puzzle piece?"

Body positioning is also important. In the midst of the budding crisis, the child wants to put distance between himself and any educator. Following the idea of making the child's most likely response the right response, when the aide hands Justin the puzzle piece, she should be standing opposite of where she wants Justin to move. Also, she should be standing just a little bit in his physical space. Justin will move to put a little space between himself and the aide. When he makes a step away from the aide, it is a step in the right direction. The aide should nod her head, letting Justin know that he made a good response. Of course, Mrs. Johnson needs to follow Justin. If he is going toward the exit, she should trail him at a short distance. If he is not moving in the right direction, she should immediately step into his physical space to prompt him to make another correct response.

The importance of skillfully making this intervention cannot be overstated. The facilitator must successfully inhibit all body language that connotes disapproval, avoid verbal directives, and keep all words to a minimum. The educator must instantly read the child's body language and make the necessary in-flight adjustments. The educator must convey approval when the child gives the first minuscule indication that he is about to make a good decision. In short, the educator must transform a situation that has all of the trappings of a lose-lose confrontation into a win-win dynamic. It takes practice.

Dealing with a Failed Plan

Often, the first plan does not work. In such cases, the failure must not be blamed on the child or the aide. Instead, blame the plan. The educator who helped the child make the first plan needs to reconvene a problem-solving session with the child. The educator should begin the meeting by saying, "Our plan did not work for us. We need to make a better one."

Key Concept

If the child does not leave the classroom as planned, the child did not fail. The plan failed.

The Importance of Sequence

When working with an oppositional child, it is tempting to start by immediately developing a plan for removing the child from the classroom when he is disruptive. Experience, which is a euphemism for making the same mistake over and over until the lesson is learned, has shown that immediately developing a plan to remove the disruptive child from the classroom is a mistake. It is a mistake because, as a first step, it has little chance of working. An oppositional child is not likely to participate in developing the plan if he does not feel physically and emotionally safe in the educator's presence. That trust has to be earned over time and hardened in the forge of adversity.

There is a second reason not to immediately make a plan to remove the child from the classroom: it might work. When such a plan works, teachers tend not to do the proactive things like environmental engineering and managing the daily antecedents. With no accommodations to promote the child's success, the initial success spurred by the plan is invariably short-lived. Furthermore, the child comes to realize that he has been manipulated, and his tendency to be oppositional hardens. (See Figure 5.2 for a Crisis Management Checklist that can help in the development of a solution that works.)

Reasons for Rejecting This Model

Not all educators who know this method of removing the child from the classroom employ it. Generally they reject it for one of four reasons: (1) fear of making an exception, (2) opposition to rewarding inappropriate behavior, (3) belief in the need for punishment, and (4) the temptation of shortcuts.

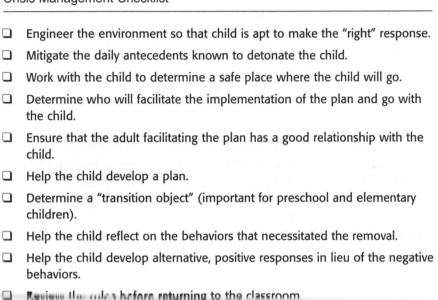

Figure 5.2
Crisis Management Checklist

❏ Engineer the environment so that child is apt to make the "right" response.

❏ Mitigate the daily antecedents known to detonate the child.

❏ Work with the child to determine a safe place where the child will go.

❏ Determine who will facilitate the implementation of the plan and go with the child.

❏ Ensure that the adult facilitating the plan has a good relationship with the child.

❏ Help the child develop a plan.

❏ Determine a "transition object" (important for preschool and elementary children).

❏ Help the child reflect on the behaviors that necessitated the removal.

❏ Help the child develop alternative, positive responses in lieu of the negative behaviors.

❏ Review the rules before returning to the classroom.

Fear of Making an Exception

Some educators do not accept the underlying premise that oppositional children should be held to a lesser standard of behavior than the other children in the classroom. They think, "If he can get away with it, they will all try to get away with it." Evidence does not bear out this attitude about children's nature. Children instinctively see their main job as becoming adults. They know immaturity when they see it, and they have no desire to purposely model it. Moreover, they understand that some children have problems, and because of these problems they need to be treated differently. Educators skillfully and successfully individualize academic instruction to accommodate the varying needs of their students. Modifying the behavioral expectations for one or two students in the classroom is only a logical extension of the practice.

Opposition to Rewarding Inappropriate Behavior

A few educators dislike this approach because, in their opinion, it "rewards" children for doing something bad. "He throws a book," they say, "and he gets rewarded by going to work on a puzzle? No way! I am not going to reward bad behavior."

Children who leave the classroom under these conditions do not feel rewarded. They know what the other children are doing. They know where they are supposed to be. They know what is normal and what is expected. There is nothing rewarding about implementing a plan to calmly leave the classroom. Furthermore, if the technique truly rewarded children for throwing a book, the rate of book throwing would markedly increase. It doesn't.

Belief in the Need for Punishment

Some educators decline to use this method for getting children to leave the classroom because they believe that if children do something wrong, they should be punished. This position stems from a deep-seated attitude about human nature. Nothing that is said here will change their mind. However, we suggest they consider data on their strategy of punishing the behavior. If their position is correct and punishment is what is needed, then the application of punishment should decrease the intensity and the frequency of these classroom disruptions. If the data show otherwise, perhaps educators should reexamine their beliefs about the value of using punishment on oppositional children—and then not use punishment.

The Temptation of Shortcuts

The intervention technique sometimes fails because, "in the interest of time," the team took a shortcut. Often, the plan isn't practiced before implementation is attempted. Demands upon educators' time, skills, and energies are endless, and there is no way to meet all of these demands. However, when the issue is developing a plan to mitigate the classroom disruptions caused by an oppositional child, no time will be saved by attempting to take a shortcut.

No One Size Fits All

The solution that works for helping one 2nd-grade child leave the classroom will not necessarily work for another 2nd-grade child who needs to leave the room, and it certainly will not work for a 6th grader. Each child requires a tailored solution. However, the basic principles are the same. The sole purpose for removing the child is to protect people from being hurt, to prevent property from being destroyed, and to ensure a viable teaching and learning environment. Yet children must be removed in a manner that ensures their dignity and does not threaten their emotional or physical safety. Any solution that meets these criteria and gets the job done is the perfect solution.

 Key Concept

Any plan that prevents the child from hurting someone, damaging property, or further disrupting the teaching and learning environment and that ensures the child's dignity is the perfect plan.

Dealing with the Crisis of a Failed Plan

It takes practice to develop and successfully implement plans that work. During this learning curve, the educator will probably have to deal with a few crises—times when the child is threatening to hurt others, to destroy property, or to seriously disrupt the learning and teaching environment. This is when it is important to remember the bottom line: the educator needs to do what is necessary, and *only* what is necessary, to prevent others from being hurt or property from being damaged. The objective of ensuring the integrity of the learning and teaching environment is, at that moment of crisis, lost. To accomplish the first two objectives—preventing others from being hurt or property from being destroyed—it is occasionally necessary to physically restrain the child.

Billy Is Out of Control

A loud crash came from the room for emotionally disturbed children. Hearing it, the school psychologist ran to the 4th-grade room. Entering it, he saw that Billy had tipped over his desk and was in the process of pulling down the blinds on the window. The school psychologist quickly restrained him.

"Billy, what work do you need to be doing now?" the school psychologist asked. Billy did not answer. Instead, he kicked at the school psychologist. But the school psychologist did nothing to hurt Billy. He only acted to prevent Billy from seriously hurting him.

"Let go of me!" Billy screamed.

"I want to, but as I do, you need to sit at your desk and read to me from your Harry Potter book," the school psychologist answered, referring to a book that Billy enjoyed.

"Then let go of me!" Billy yelled again. The school psychologist relaxed his grip on Billy and slowly released him. Billy took three steps toward his desk, which the aide had set back upright, but then grabbed a computer keyboard and started to throw it. Instantly, the school psychologist grabbed both of Billy's arms. The struggle was on again. After a minute, Billy again ordered, "Let go of me!"

"I want to, Billy," the school psychologist repeated. "But you must be able to control yourself. If I let go, you need to sit at your desk and do something that interests you—anything."

"I can't," Billy said, tears streaming to his face. "Can you help me?"

This vignette illustrates several points. First, the child cannot be permitted to destroy property. Occasionally, physical intervention is needed as a last resort. Second, during the crisis it does not help to tell the child to stop destroying things. For example, the school psychologist did not say, "Billy, stop trying to pull the blinds off of the wall." Instead, the educator needs to direct the child to an appropriate activity. Finally, despite his behavior, the child's safety was not endangered, and he was not punished or threatened with punishment.

Dealing with the Child Who Wants a Confrontation

Occasionally, a child seems to set out to provoke a confrontation. The child might push a book off his desk so that it crashes loudly to the floor. The loud noise temporarily disrupts a few students' learning, but the incident is over. It can, the teacher concludes, be ignored. Then the child grabs his pencil and breaks it with a loud snap. Again, the teacher ignores it, but she is now watching him out of the corner of her eye. Then, before the teacher can do anything to prevent it, the student jumps up and tips over his desk. This student not only wants a confrontation, but the purposefulness of the behavior suggests that he will not be amenable to implementing his plan to leave the room. Nonetheless, the plan should be offered and the child should be given an opportunity to make a good decision. If he does not, which he probably won't, the teacher has no alternative but to use the level of intervention required to protect people's safety and property and to ensure the integrity of the teaching and learning environment.

Application to Cassandra

Because Cassandra had no behaviors that necessitated removing her from the classroom, there was no need for her to develop a plan.

Application to Harry

Harry lost control in the face of two different types of situations. He often lost control of his emotions during unsupervised activities, such as the transition from class to class as he and the other students walked through the hallways. He also could lose control of his emotions in the classroom. Each of these two problems required a different solution.

Hallway Problems

Each altercation in the hallway followed the same scenario. Harry would make a snide comment or insult another boy, and the boy would verbally challenge Harry. Harry would take a swing or give him a push. Almost every time, Harry came out on the losing end of the fight, but getting beat up did not deter him from fighting again. Of course, beating up Harry became a badge of honor among the boys. Without a doubt, Harry was a victim of bullying. However, boys who never bullied anyone else got into fights with Harry.

Having Harry remain in the classroom while the other students went to their classes decreased the frequency of hallway disruptions. Then Harry went to the next class just a few minutes before the bell.

Classroom Disruptions

The frequency of the classroom disruptions decreased when, as discussed in Chapter 4, the proactive antecedents were put in place. However, Harry continued to disturb some classes occasionally. At these times, a directive from the teacher for an appropriate behavior did not work. It only seemed to confirm to Harry that he had successfully pushed the teacher's emotional button.

It was decided that when Harry seemed determined to disrupt the class, he would be given an "errand." The teacher would remember an important letter that had to be delivered to the office, to Mr. Adams in the resource room, or to the counselor. She would ask Harry to be the errand boy. Most of these messages were authentic, but none were urgent. It took Harry about five minutes to deliver the message and return to class. This brief change in routine was sufficient to break his mind-set, and by then the class had settled down. Children were no longer snickering and giggling. The class had moved on, and Harry needed to sit quietly and pay attention so that he could get back into the flow of things. In other words, the intervention accomplished its objective. It successfully restored the teaching and learning environment, and it preserved Harry's dignity.

6

Providing Services at School

Teachers who have a child with oppositional behaviors in their classroom need help. Make no mistake about that! Moreover, when these children finish one grade and move to the next, any and every proven strategy needs to go with them. This suggests special education services, and that is an issue that merits discussion.

Since 1975, the federal government has allotted money so that schools can provide an appropriate education in the least restrictive setting to children with disabilities. However, always mindful of tax money, Congress attached strings. In order for a school to get these monies, the child has to fit into one of 14 "categories."[a] One of the categories is for children who have a serious emotional disturbance (SED). To qualify for SED services, a child must meet the following criteria:[1]

The condition must exhibit one or more of the following characteristics over a long period of time and to a marked degree which adversely affects educational performance:

A. An inability to learn that cannot be explained by intellectual, sensory, or other health factors;

B. An inability to build or maintain satisfactory interpersonal relationships with peers and teachers;

C. Inappropriate types of behavior or feelings under normal circumstances;

D. A general pervasive mood of unhappiness or depression;

E. A tendency to develop physical symptoms or fears associated with personal or school problems.

The key for qualifying children with conduct problems for services under the SED label is whether their behavior adversely affects their educational performance. Arguably, children's educational performance is adversely affected if they are not completing work, have difficulty participating in cooperative-learning tasks, or are often out of the classroom and missing instruction because of discipline problems. Many oppositional children qualify. The first step toward qualification is doing a comprehensive multidisciplinary assessment—a composite evaluation of the child based on independently done assessments by two or more professionals. For instance, the special education teacher might give the child an individually administered test of his academic skills, the speech and language pathologist might determine the child's expressive communication skills, and the social worker might rate the child's adaptive skills. A multidisciplinary assessment must, by statute, include a classroom observation among its components. The value of a proper assessment is that several specialists independently evaluate the child and then examine their findings for consistency and completeness to collectively determine a child's education needs.

 Key Concept

Many children with conduct problems qualify for special services, and they often need them.

The Multidisciplinary Assessment Meeting

Purpose

The child's education team, which includes the parents, meets to share and to discuss the assessment results. If the team adheres to best practices, this is the first time that any one member of the team has heard the assessment results and the opinions of the team members. Typically, their collective findings include minor but important discrepancies. It is necessary to reconcile these apparent discrepancies, and the parents often have key information that explains away these seemingly contradictory findings and gives a richer, more textured understanding of the child. Of course, the uncooked presentation of the results by itself encourages the parents to participate in the meeting and, in a meaningful way, to become members of the team.

When a consensus is reached, the results determine whether the child qualifies for services, and they also shed light on the child's educational needs. On the basis of these identified needs, the team determines the services that are necessary to meet the child's educational needs. At a minimum, the intended learning or behavior objectives for each service should be outlined.

Participants

The makeup of the meeting varies depending on the professionals called on to contribute to the assessment, and the composition also varies by specialists who might be asked to deliver the services. However, every meeting has certain core participants: the parents, an administrator, and the child's classroom teacher. Such specialists as the school psychologist, the speech and language therapist, the physical therapist, an audiologist, or a learning disabilities specialist might also attend. Each participant has a specific role.

Parents. The most important persons at the meeting are the parents. Federal statute underscores the importance of their role. No meeting, regardless of what it might be called, may be held to make binding decisions about altering the child's educational programming without at least one of the child's parents in attendance.

The parents have an exceptionally difficult role. First, they are the only laypeople at the meeting. Everyone else is a professional educator who has had years of training. The parents are also the strangers at the table. The educators all know each other well and work together daily. Finally, the meetings are always held at the school. It is the educators' turf. But these issues pale in comparison with the really tough issue. The meeting was called because the child is having "behavior problems," a phrase that seems synonymous with "misbehavior." To the parents, it seems as though everyone at the table knows why the child is misbehaving—poor parenting.

The parents must accept that they have only limited control over their child's behavior. More important, they have to acknowledge that everyone at the meeting is there to help the child be successful in school. To enhance their objectivity, parents should come to the meeting with their concerns and suggestions written out and then stick to their script.

The parents also need to become the child's case managers. Schooling is a 12-year process. During that time, the child will have many teachers, will be seen by numbers of specialists, will be given countless evaluations, and will probably have three different principals. The only constant in this kaleidoscope of people in the child's educational life is the parents. They need to immediately start collecting and organizing the pertinent information about the child in a binder or other organizational tool. Parents have a right to review any information in anyone's file at school, and they can make copies to keep in their case-management binder.

Teacher. Of all the members of the professional team, the teacher has the most difficult role. The teacher has to deal with a child who sometimes endangers people's safety, who frequently disrupts others' learning, and who constantly needs prompts to keep on task. Any teacher who is committed to enhancing the learning and social development of every student in the class cannot help but feel frustration, stress, and even anger toward this time-demanding child. Although these feelings are completely understandable, they are counterproductive. It is important that the teacher finds a good listener (such as the school counselor or the school psychologist) and, as needed, vents those feelings.

When it comes to changing the child's behavior, the heavy lifting is left to the classroom teacher. On her own, the child has almost no capacity to change her behavior. She never "willed" herself to be bad, and despite admonishments from others and her own best intentions, she cannot change her behavior. In the classroom, only one person has the capacity to change, and that is the teacher. If the child is going to become less oppositional and more compliant, it is the teacher who must initially do something different.

Principal. At some schools, the administrator sends a designee to the meeting. However, federal statutes require that an administrator attend, and the parents should politely insist on it. The administrator, usually the building principal, is there because she is the designated keeper of the school's resources. In theory, the team decides what resources are necessary to meet the child's needs, and it is incumbent upon the administration to provide those resources. But theory is saluted only in the courtroom, and law libraries could be wallpapered with decrees from judges telling school administrators that they will, despite their dearth of funds, spend the money needed to meet a particular child's needs. In practice, the school stretches its limited resources as far as possible to do the best job it can to meet the educational needs of all the children. However, in the case of Cassandra, for example, Cassandra's mother is interested only in seeing to it that the principal does not veto needed services for Cassandra "because the school can't afford it." Parents' mere awareness of this dynamic is usually sufficient to ensure that the school does not balance its special education budget at their child's expense.

The principal also manages, allocates, and coordinates people. If the team decides that an aide is needed, it is the principal's job to procure one. If the team decides that the child needs the services of the learning disabilities teacher, the speech and language therapist, and the school counselor, then the principal must work with these professionals to coordinate the provision of the needed services.

School Psychologist. The school psychologist has multiple responsibilities. She is usually the person who does the classroom observation, synthesizes the results, and presents the findings to the multidisciplinary team. When the assessment supports categorizing the child as being seriously emotionally disturbed, the school psychologist is apt to be the person who gathers the findings from other team members and writes the composite evaluation summary. After the meeting, the school psychologist sets up procedures for routinely collecting data to monitor whether progress is being made toward the child's learning and behavioral objectives. If, after a reasonable period of time, say six weeks, there is no change in the target behaviors, the team needs to reconvene to address the problem.

Also, the school psychologist is the mental health professional on the team. As such, she shares information (given proper releases from the parents) and communicates with health professionals in the private sector, particularly the family physician or child psychiatrist.

Language Therapist. Prevalence studies have found that a high percentage of children with conduct problems also have language problems.[2] Furthermore, evidence indicates that symptom-targeted language therapy is useful.[3] As our understanding of the language deficits of behaviorally disturbed children increases, we can expect that language therapists will increasingly be providing their services to children with conduct problems.

 Key Concept

Many children with conduct problems also have a communication disorder that responds to language therapy.

School Counselor. School is not just about enhancing children's academic skills. School is also about equipping children with the social skills they need to find a niche within the broader society. That is to say, school is also about learning how to get along with others. At school, children need two sets of social skills. They need one set to have positive relationships with their peers, and they need another set to have positive relationships with the adults in the school—primarily their teacher. For example, 1st-grade students need such generic peer-relationship skills as sharing, playing cooperatively, and taking turns. To get along with their teacher, children need the social skills of listening, complying with directives, and following classroom rules.

Typically, school counselors instruct all children in generic socialization skills. In addition, some school counselors are increasingly providing more intense social-skill training for at-risk children.

Designating a Parent-Support Person

Most parents of oppositional children feel alienated, disenfranchised, and guilty. Parents who come to the meeting wearing those feelings on their sleeve are likely to take one of two postures. Either they will avoid eye contact and meekly nod in concurrence with everything that is said, or they will come to the meeting bristling with anger and ready to argue at the first suggestion that their child causes any more classroom problems than the next child. Both postures are understandable, but they are not useful. Any meeting that begins with a parent consumed with those feelings is launching into stormy weather.

Key Concept

It is critical that the parents contribute to the team's problem-solving process; but for this to happen, the school needs to give special attention to the parents' concerns.

To increase the chances of a successful meeting, one of the educators on the team should be the designated parent-support person. The best parent-support person is the team member who, in the parents' eyes, wears the whitest hat. This usually eliminates anyone who has had to convey unpleasant news to the parents or had to intervene when the child was out of control. The best candidates are the school counselor, the school psychologist, or the speech and language therapist.

The parent-support person should contact the parents before the meeting via a letter (see the sample letter in Figure 6.1). The letter should give a brief overview of the purpose of the meeting, lay out the agenda, identify the participants, and state that the parents will soon receive a phone call to set a time for the meeting.

Figure 6.1
Sample Letter Inviting Parent to an Assessment Meeting

Dear Mrs. Curl:

The assessment of Cassandra's learning abilities and her behavior in comparison to other children her age has been completed. It is now time for Cassandra's educational team to meet and discuss the results and their implications for Cassandra's educational programming. In addition to yourself and whomever you might like to accompany you to the meeting, the following people will be at the meeting:

- Mrs. Sommers, principal
- Ms. Jones, Cassandra's 3rd-grade teacher
- Mr. Peterson, school psychologist
- Mrs. Abbot, speech and language therapist
- Mr. Dalton, learning disabilities teacher

I will phone you on Thursday, October 5, to confer with you as to a time that is convenient for you to attend the meeting. According to school records, your home phone number is 845-2067. If that number is not correct or if I will not be able to reach you at that number, please contact me. My school phone number is 845-3972, extension 16. If I am not at my phone, please leave a voicemail message giving me a time and phone number for contacting you.

The agenda for the meeting is as follows:

- Review the assessment findings.
- Determine whether Cassandra's educational needs are being adequately met.
- Determine whether there is a need for additional services.
- Determine whether Cassandra is eligible for additional services.
- Identify the types of special services, if any, that will be provided.
- Outline the learning and behavior objectives expected from any additional services.

Mrs. Curl, I look forward to meeting you and working with you for Cassandra's educational benefit.

Sincerely,

Joe Peterson, School Psychologist

When making the call, the parent-support person should try to find a time for the meeting that allows both parents to attend. The parent-support person should also ask the parents if there is anything that will make it difficult for them to attend the meeting. If child care is a problem, the parent-support person should offer the school's services (meaning a classroom aide or a parent volunteer will provide child care during the meeting). Even if the parents do not mention child care, the parent-support person should make sure that child care is available. Many meetings have been doomed at the outset because the parents brought a 3-year-old to the meeting or expected the target child to wait patiently in the car until "Mommy and Daddy are ready."

The parent-support person must not preview the meeting with the parents. If questioned too closely about issues that will be discussed at the meeting, the parent-support person should say something like this: "The questions you are raising are important; however, everyone at the meeting, including you, will want to contribute to the answer. Rather than answer questions that are best addressed by the entire team, I can help you develop a list of the questions that you can expect to get answered at the meeting." By this point, the parent-support person has assessed the parents' level of anxiety and insecurity. If it is high, the parent-support person should offer to hold a pre-conference with the parents so they can develop that list of questions. While developing the list of questions, they are building trust, and at these meetings, trust is critical.

If there is any remaining concern about the parents' level of confidence, the parent-support person should offer to put them in contact with a parent who is successfully raising a child who is receiving special services. To form this alliance, the parent-support person might say, "Mrs. Curl, I know a parent who has been in the same situation where you now find yourself. She, too, has a child who works hard to find success at school and needs extra assistance. Her name is Lois Grant. Mrs. Curl, with your permission I will ask Mrs. Grant to give you a phone call. She knows the ropes, and you'll find her most helpful. Can I ask Mrs. Grant to contact you?" The value of this parent alliance cannot be overstated. Every school should have a Mrs. Grant.

On the day of the meeting, the parent-support person must make sure that the educators don't end up literally on one side of the table and the parents and any accompanying support person, such as Mrs. Grant, on the other side. Also, the seating arrangement must ensure that the parent is not sitting out of the normal communication loop. Of course, the parent-support person sits next to the parents.

Facilitating the Meeting

It is important to explicitly tell the parents that they have an important contribution to make to the team's understanding of the child. This message is nicely conveyed by a facilitator who may begin the meeting by saying something like the following.

An Excerpt from Cassandra's Meeting

Many of us here at the table are knowledgeable about various aspects of children's learning and behavior, and we have that knowledge base to help us understand Cassandra. But with the exception of Ms. Jones, who has known Cassandra for several months but only in the school setting, many of us have known Cassandra for only the couple of hours it took to do our various evaluations. In contrast, Mrs. Curl, you have known Cassandra for all of her 10 years, 3 months, and 27 days. We educators know a lot about children's learning and behavior, but you are the expert on Cassandra. It is important that we pool our knowledge to obtain the best understanding of Cassandra's strengths and her educational needs.

At these meetings it is tempting to affix blame. After all, there is a problem, and therefore someone has to be at fault (or so the perverse logic goes). Often it is the child who gets blamed. Even Cassandra's mother might say, "I just don't know why Cassandra is so bad in school." When hearing the language of blame, the facilitator must immediately reframe the statement. So in response to Cassandra's mother and before anyone else can comment, the facilitator needs to say, "Mrs. Curl, are you wondering why Cassandra doesn't finish her desk assignments? Joe [addressing the school psychologist], was there anything in the classroom observation that might give us insight into that?" When the teacher turns to Mrs. Curl and says, "Does Cassandra get away with that kind of thing at home?" the facilitator must redirect the focus back to school issues. He might say, "Mrs. Curl, what discipline techniques have you found effective at home that might work for us at school when Cassandra folds her arms across her chest and refuses to do anything?" If the principal asks the teacher, "Why did Cassandra go so long before it was determined that she was significantly behind in reading?" the facilitator needs to say, "I hear you wondering what coping skills Cassandra uses to accommodate for her delay in reading."

Dealing with the Labeling Issue

Many parents cringe at the idea of the school labeling their child as SED. Some parents would prefer that their child went without services rather than "get stuck with that label." Therefore, it is incumbent on educators to approach the parents' concerns with sensitivity, compassion, and skill.

When meeting with parents to discuss whether their child qualifies for SED services, it is not wise to begin the meeting by talking about the child's label. Rather, the team should first discuss whether anyone has concerns about the child's educational performance. Once the child's educational concerns are specified, the team should consider the array of services that are needed to meet the child's identified needs. These services might include putting an aide in the classroom with primary responsibility for the child, having the child attend social skills training, scheduling time with the language therapist, and so on. Generally, and almost without exception, parents will agree that their child needs these services. Then it is time to approach the delicate issue of "the label." It might be handled like this:

"Labeling" Cassandra

"Let me summarize," the facilitator said. "The team has agreed that the evaluations and the classroom observations indicate concerns about Cassandra's schoolwork. Specifically, Cassandra is having problems completing desk assignments; she has trouble participating with her peers on cooperative-learning tasks; she does not know many of the multiplication and division facts; and she often misses instructional time because she is out of the room due to her behavior. So the team is saying that Cassandra needs special services. Specifically, the team would like Cassandra to have an aide. The aide would help Cassandra stay on task when doing independent work, provide guidance during cooperative-learning tasks, and direct Cassandra's attention during instructional times. The team feels that Cassandra would benefit from social skills training. Finally, the team would like a special educator to help Cassandra with her reading and to fill in some missing math skills. Is that an accurate summary of Cassandra's needs and the services that the team recommends?" The team members nodded in agreement.

"Okay, that leaves us with just one issue—determining whether Cassandra fits into one of the 14 categories. Mrs. Curl," the facilitator said, turning toward Cassandra's mother, "not every child in school is eligible for special services. The federal government, which provides the money, allows us to dispense special services only to children who qualify. To qualify for special services is like having a ticket to the dance, and in education there are 14 different-colored tickets to the dance. For example, children who have autism get a ticket, maybe a blue one, so that they can get the services that meet their needs. But I haven't heard anyone on the team suggest that Cassandra has autism, so she cannot be given a blue ticket. Children who are mentally retarded also get a ticket that gives them access to special services, but Cassandra is not mentally retarded, and if the team classified her as such in order to get special services, the school would risk failing their next review from the state. However, there is one category for which Cassandra seems to qualify. That category is for children whose academic performance is affected by interpersonal relationship problems with peers and teachers and who often display inappropriate behavior under normal circumstances. Based on the evaluations and what has been said, it seems that Cassandra meets the criteria for getting special services under the Serious Emotional Disturbance category. Does the team feel that Cassandra meets the criteria for Serious Emotional Disturbance and therefore qualifies for services?"

Referral to a Pediatric Psychiatrist

Children can be aggressive and antisocial for myriad reasons. Boys who are clinically depressed are often irritable and aggressive. Children who have Generalized Anxiety Disorder are typically hypervigilant and easily distracted. They often do not complete assignments and do not pay sufficient attention to social cues to properly interpret them. Children with mild autism become aggressive when their routine changes. Children with Asperger's Syndrome have trouble correctly interpreting social cues and interacting with their peers. Out of frustration, they sometimes respond with aggression. Children with Fragile X Syndrome are hyperactive and easily agitated, and sometimes self-abusive. And the list goes on. The point is that any child who qualifies for special education programming because of behavior problems needs to be seen by a pediatric psychiatrist. In some cases, the child's root problem is not oppositional behaviors. A correct diagnosis can direct the team toward appropriate and fruitful educational programming.

However, any referral to a private provider needs to be handled carefully. If the referral is being made for educational reasons, the school is financially responsible. The line between health needs and family responsibilities on the one hand and educational needs and school obligations on the other is not clearly drawn. Although it is important that the child be seen by a child psychiatrist to get an accurate diagnosis of the underlying disorder, the school should be careful about using language that connotes financial responsibility. Also, as a publicly funded institution, the school needs to steer clear of the temptation to recommend one private practitioner over another.

Potential Benefits of Language Therapy

To the best of our knowledge, there is no significant body of research that explores effective therapy techniques for conduct-disordered children with language problems, and there are no commercially available therapy materials or curriculum materials. However, based on our experience with many of these children, we offer what should be considered a first approximation of approaches that might be useful.

Application to Justin

Justin had a deficit in his expressive language skills. Like many children with conduct problems, he had few words with which to label his feelings or the feelings of others. When children can label only two emotions, happy and angry, they tend to spend a lot of time being angry.

The language therapist started by helping Justin associate feelings with situations. Justin was asked to choose the correct word to complete a series of statements with accompanying picture cards:

- The teacher is standing with her arms crossed and a frown on her face. She is (happy) (angry).

- When John opened his present and found that the box was empty, he felt (sad) (happy).

- Amy made the winning basket, and she was (confused) (happy).

- When Tom's bike tire went flat, he was (happy) (surprised).

- Bill wanted to go outside and play, but it was raining. He was (disappointed) (mad).

Next, the language therapist posed situations for Justin and asked him to match them with an emotion. For example, the language therapist said, "Justin, there are two seconds left in the basketball game, and the score is tied. You shoot and you make the winning basket. You feel _____." Or "Justin, don't look under your desk, but there is a king cobra lying down there and it is looking at your big toe. You feel _____." Then they alternated roles, and Justin posed a situation and the language therapist had to match it with an emotion that, in Justin's opinion, fit. Following this exercise, Justin had to note one thing he experienced each day and draw a picture showing how it made him feel. After a week, he and the therapist discussed his daily notes.

The language therapist then asked Justin to complete a chart to keep track of his emotions (see Figure 6.2). His assignment was to

Figure 6.2
Chart for Recording Emotions

Day	Sad	Mad	Glad	Scared	Blah
Monday					
Tuesday					
Wednesday					
Thursday					
Friday					

record each time during the day that he felt any of these emotions and to make a notation in the cell that would remind him of the situation that had elicited the feeling. For example, if he was sent to the principal's office on Tuesday and he felt scared, he might put a P under "Scared," and it would remind him when he felt scared in the principal's office. Each day Justin was to note at least three different feelings he had experienced. When he came to language therapy, Justin showed his chart to the therapist, and they discussed the situations that had elicited each recorded feeling. The therapist asked Justin questions designed to get him in touch with the physical symptoms and thoughts associated with each emotion. For example, she asked, "Justin, when you were sitting in the principal's office waiting for her, do you recall what your heart was doing? Were you sweating? Was your stomach upset? Did you bite your fingernails? What thoughts were going through your head?" Then, looking at all of the associated symptoms, she and Justin tried to determine if he had correctly labeled the feeling. They did this for two weeks.

Justin's next assignment was to look at pictures of different people that the therapist had cut out of magazines and guess, based on the context and the person's facial expressions and gestures, what emotion each person was feeling at that moment. For his next assignment, Justin and the therapist walked around the school and watched people from a distance. On the basis of the person's facial expressions and gestures, they discussed what each person might be feeling. Finally, Justin was given the assignment of using feeling words to express his emotions when he was having difficulty with a peer. If his teacher happened to observe the interaction, she later gave Justin feedback on his ability to tell the peer how he was feeling.

Application to Cassandra

Assessments revealed that Cassandra had a mixed communication language disorder. Observation and informal assessments indicated that, among other language deficits, Cassandra had limited capacity to generate behavior-regulating thought. For example, Cassandra was shown this drawing:

Pointing to the rows of squares, the examiner asked, "Cassandra, if these were cookies, which row has more cookies—the top row or the bottom row?"

"The bottom row," Cassandra replied, running her finger from one end of the line to the other. Cassandra "sees" more cookies in the bottom row because these circles take up more space. According to Piaget, Cassandra was operating at the sensory-motor stage of cognitive development, when "more" was determined by her senses.[4] But Cassandra was in the 3rd grade, and most 3rd graders are in the concrete stage of cognitive development. They use logic to override their senses. So the examiner said, "Cassandra, show me that the bottom row has more cookies than the top row." Cassandra put her finger on each cookie (square) in each row, counted out loud, and then said, "Oh. The top row has more cookies." When given a verbal prompt that required her to "think" (for example, use behavior-regulating thought), Cassandra moved from the sensory-motor stage to the concrete stage.

We have observed that many children with oppositional and defiant behaviors remain at the sensory-motor stage longer than other children of similar age and mental ability.[b] We have also observed that many oppositional children have more difficulty than other children of comparable age and mental ability at changing response sets. Their inflexibility at shifting response sets is particularly apparent when they do math operations. Cassandra could add and subtract three-digit numbers—as long as each type of operation was on a different page. When both operations were interspersed on the same page, she made many errors. It was difficult for her to shift response sets, which, again, is a task that requires behavior-regulating thought.

The speech and language therapist provided a series of activities designed to promote the development of Cassandra's behavior-regulating thought. First, the therapist and Cassandra played "Simon

Says" activities. For example, Simon says, "Stand up." Simon says, "Blink your right eye," and so on. To keep the child engaged, the therapist occasionally said something like "Simon says, 'Pick up the cup,'" and under the cup Cassandra found an M&M. By design, the Simon Says activity mirrored how, according to A. R. Luria, mothers instill behavior-regulating thought in their children.[5]

Next, the therapist added directives that Cassandra often heard and occasionally refused to follow in the classroom. For example, Simon says, "Put your reading book away," or Simon says, "Get out your math workbook," or Simon says, "Sit down."

For exercise three, the therapist put in a time delay. For example, Simon says, "Complete this math sheet (which was below Cassandra's academic level) and then give me your pencil." Gradually, the time delays were lengthened. For example, at the beginning of the session the therapist might say, "Cassandra, remind me that at the end of the session I want to give you something." Cassandra had to keep that thought on her mind all during the session and then, when the session was over, remind the therapist to give her something.

Exercise four consisted of two-step directions. For example, the therapist could have said, "Simon says, 'Stand on your left foot and raise your right hand,'" or "I say, do two more problems on the math sheet and then put it on my desk."

For the last exercise, Cassandra was given two different objects, such as a red pencil and a blue pencil, and told to do the opposite of what the therapist said. So when the therapist said, "Give me the *red* pencil," Cassandra was to hand her the blue pencil. If the therapist said, "Give me the *small* ball," Cassandra was to give her the big ball. This was then extended to activities that did not have an object representation. When the therapist said, "Cassandra, *sit down*," Cassandra was to stand up. When the therapist said, "Cassandra, stand on your *right* foot," Cassandra was to stand on her left foot. In these two exercises, Cassandra had to translate the requests into different messages. This could be accomplished only by generating behavior-regulating thought.

When children learn skills in one setting, they do not readily generalize those skills to other settings.[6] To achieve generalization, students need to (1) apply the skill in the target setting, (2) self-monitor their performance, and (3) get supportive but also corrective feedback.[7] Therefore, the language therapist gave Cassandra homework assignments. The first homework assignment required Cassandra to apply the skill of following requests in the classroom. For one week, Cassandra completed the chart in Figure 6.3.

On this chart, Cassandra wrote down the first directive Ms. Jones gave after the designated time and then recorded whether she followed the request. To get the "game" started, Ms. Jones initially gave Cassandra some playful requests. For example, on Monday at 9 o'clock Ms. Jones privately said to Cassandra, "Look in the cup on my desk and, without anyone seeing you doing it, put whatever you find in the cup in your pocket." Under the cup was a piece of candy. At the end of the week, Cassandra and the language therapist reviewed the chart and discussed it. The activity continued for three weeks, with the teacher using increasingly valid classroom instructions.

Application to Harry

Harry had a receptive language deficit. More precisely, he had problems with pragmatics; that is, he had difficulty getting the "true" meaning from everyday conversations. He listened solely to the words of the communication and failed to take into consideration who was saying it, the speaker's intonation, or the accompanying nonverbal expressions. Therefore, he often took communications too literally. For example, when Joe, a classmate, said, "Harry, it's all over school that Susie has a crush on you," Harry didn't note Joe's devilish smirk; he failed to recall that Joe was known for his malicious teasing; and he didn't consider that Susie had never given him any indication that she liked him. So Harry was stunned and confused when he asked Susie to the school dance that coming Friday evening and she flatly declined.

Impaired pragmatics also affected Harry's relationship with his teachers. According to Harry, other students could make a smart remark and the teacher would laugh or teasingly say, "Ah, knock it off." But, in Harry's view, when he said the same thing, the teacher blew up and gave him after-school detention.

Figure 6.3
Chart for Self-Monitoring Compliance with Classroom Requests

Day	Time	Teacher Request	YES	NO
Monday	9:00			
Tuesday	10:00			
Wednesday	11:00			
Thursday	1:00			
Friday	2:00			

Harry needed instruction in using all of the available clues to decode oral communications. The language therapist collected pictures from magazines of various well-known people such as Pope John Paul II, President George W. Bush, and actor Tom Cruise, and wrote out statements made by each of them. Harry's task was to match the picture with statements each person had made. Then the language therapist selected movies and played scenes from each movie without the sound. Harry's task was to look at the actors' body language, facial expressions, and gestures, and, from numerous options, select the right script.

The language therapist then gave Harry his first assignment. Each day for one week he was to look at a person, and, using the chart in Figure 6.4, write down their statement and describe their concurrent facial expression, body language, and gestures. He did this for the first person who talked after the start of each hour.

Harry's next assignment was to observe certain people at specific times of the day and note what they were probably feeling, using the form in Figure 6.5.

On Tuesday at 10:00, Harry observed the teacher monitoring the hall; on Wednesday at 11:00, he observed Joe, a classmate, during physical education; on Thursday at 2:00, Harry observed Susie, another classmate, during art; and on Friday at 3:40, he observed the principal monitoring the students getting on the school buses.

Harry's final assignment was to pay attention to oral communications directed to him and to determine their "true" message. The conversation did not have to be more than a sentence or two. Harry made notations about the spoken message and also the person's facial expression, body language, and gestures, and combined all of the clues into his understanding of the oral communication. Immediately after school, he stopped by the language therapist's office and they discussed his findings.

Social Skills Training

Getting along with others does not happen by chance or even because of a winsome smile. Rather, people who get along with others have identifiable social skills. Most children acquire social skills in the

Figure 6.4
Chart for Recording Nonverbal Communication

Day	Time	Sentence	Facial Expression	Gesture	Body Language
Monday	9:00				
Tuesday	10:00				
Wednesday	11:00				
Thursday	1:00				
Friday	2:00				

Figure 6.5
Form for Recording Feelings

Day: _____ Time: _____

Person Observed: _____

Activity: _____

Gestures: _____

Facial Expression: _____

Probably Feeling: _____

normal course of development. But some do not. When children lack social skills, they are at risk for being aggressive, for being rejected by their peers, and for developing serious conduct problems.[8] Social skills training assumes that children can be taught how to develop and maintain positive relationships with peers and teachers. Several approaches have been taken to inculcate social skills, including operant conditioning techniques.[9] However, cognitive-behavior training is the most commonly used technique because, in part, teachers support that approach,[10] and the research has found that antisocial children have faulty perceptions of social interactions, limited ability to discern subtle social cues, and distorted thinking about the dynamics of interpersonal relationships.[11] One of the appealing attributes of social skills training is that it does not focus directly on the child's problematic behavior, but instead focuses on increasing the frequency of prosocial behaviors.

Key Concept

Social skills training should be provided to all children who have conduct problems and qualify for special services.

Most cognitive-behavior social skills training follows four sequenced steps.[12] The steps are (1) instruction, (2) rehearsal, (3) feedback and reinforcement, and (4) reductive processes. In the instruction step, the coach defines the skill, explains the importance of the skill, and talks about how the skill is executed. For example, if the skill is making eye contact, the coach might explain to a small group of 6-year-old children that when you want to talk to a person, you first look at their eyes. Your eye contact, he explains, lets the person know that you are about to say something. When the person is ready to listen, he returns the eye contact. When the person you want to talk to has returned the eye contact, you can start talking. During the instruction step, modeling is frequently used to help explain the skill. Children, in particular, learn best by watching a skill being modeled.[13] Modeling is even more effective when the people shown performing the skill are of the same gender and of a similar age as the child.[14]

Behavior rehearsal, or practice, is the next step. The children need to role-play the skill in situations that are progressively more environmentally valid. So the first role-play might be with the trainer. For example, each child might be given the opportunity to say, "Hi," but the child has to wait until the trainer has returned the child's effort to make eye contact. The next step might be having the children work in pairs to implement the skill following scripts. Then the children might engage in play and, while playing, practice the skills. The end goal is for the children to implement the skill (in this case, making eye contact before talking) in their daily interactions with peers and adults at school.

Reinforcement and feedback start with behavior rehearsal. The children are reinforced for their effort and given specific feedback on their execution of the skill. During the role-plays, reinforcement (i.e., praise) and feedback can be via coaching from the trainer. During implementation, it is essential that the children continue to get reinforcement for their efforts to implement the skill and feedback on their performance. There is great value in having the children self-monitor the implementation of the target skill and report their performance back to the coach, who provides reinforcement and feedback.

Self-monitoring is important because it keeps the children aware of the skill and actively monitoring their social environment for the right time to implement the skill. Finally, the teacher and other appropriate personnel should periodically observe each child implement the skill in the classroom and give the child reinforcement and feedback.

Children can have social skills deficits for two different reasons: (1) they can't do them (an acquisition deficit), or (2) they won't do them (a performance deficit).[15] For most children, the absence of a social skill is due to a performance deficit, and most performance deficits occur because of the presence of an interfering problem behavior.[12] Reductive procedures are used to decrease the frequency of the interfering problem behaviors. Reductive procedures include response cost (such as taking away a child's recess for talking), overcorrection (such as telling a child who draws on his desk that, after school, he must wash all of the desks), and differential reinforcement of other behaviors (such as giving a reinforcement token to a child after every five consecutive minutes he sits at his desk).[16] However, two of these reductive techniques involve punishment. For reasons that will be explained, we caution punishing children.

Social skills training has a long history.[17] However, its effectiveness has been questioned,[18] and it has even been described as a promise unfulfilled[19] because the effects of social skills training are often short-lived and fail to become generalized.[20] However, when carefully planned and implemented, social skills training can be effective.[21,22] The keys are to do the following:

- Target at-risk children.[23]
- Address specific target behaviors the child needs in the classroom.[24]
- Train for a substantial amount of time, probably over the course of the school year.[25]
- Have the child do personal goal setting and contingency contracts.[26]
- Require the child to self-monitor performance of the skill.[26]

- Provide for ongoing supportive and corrective feedback from educators.[27]
- Follow up with booster sessions.[20]

Having a Designated Space

Form dictates function. That architectural axiom is also true for school buildings. Space determines how children are served, and the lack of space often means that children with conduct problems are not well served. In the "old" days, a teacher could send a student who hadn't behaved properly to the principal's office and expect that the student would quietly sit—trembling, of course—across from the secretary while waiting to be seen by the principal. The student suddenly became an angel hoping that a show of good behavior would avert a phone call to her parents. The only space needed was a secretary's office with a place to put an empty chair. In a pinch, the child sometimes sat quietly in a chair placed in the hallway.

Those were the old days. Today, a child who has been removed from a classroom may come into the principal's office out of control. If shown a chair in the principal's office, he is more apt to throw it than to sit in it. Even if he can see the principal immediately, the problem is not solved. In the principal's office, he will likely shove the papers off her desk or push over a bookcase. Under these circumstances, educators are forced to resort to physical restraint or other highly coercive techniques in order to prevent the child from hurting himself or others, destroying property, or making it look to the public as though the school is a zoo and the principal is the zookeeper.

The answer is space. These temporarily out-of-control children need some place to go where they cannot endanger others, destroy property, or hurt themselves. To be specific, every school should have one or two 12-foot-square rooms equipped with a one-way mirror, an intercom piped to the office, and a door that can be locked from the inside with a slide lock near the top. This is a space where an aide can take Justin for a half hour when he needs to leave the classroom to calm himself by putting together his puzzle. It is a space where occasionally a child needs to spend several days working one-on-one with a skilled educator to learn the self-control skills needed to function in the classroom. It is a space where a child needs to go for the last couple of hours of every school day for perhaps as long as a semester because he just cannot hold it together in the classroom those last two hours of the day. It is a space where the school psychologist or the school counselor can work one-on-one with a child while modeling and training an aide in the fine points of implementing specific behavior techniques with a particular child. Without this type of space available for their temporary short-term use, educators cannot meet the needs of many children who could otherwise be served successfully in school.

Conclusion

Many children who display oppositional and defiant behaviors or other forms of antisocial behavior at school qualify for special education services under the SED category. Because of the stigma that is commonly attached to behavior disorders, it is necessary for educators to be particularly sensitive to the parents' concerns. They also need to go to extra lengths to help the parents become full-fledged members of the child's education team. Qualifying a child for special services provides many advantages. In addition to the typical array of special education services, schools should consider whether the child would benefit from language therapy and intensive social skills training.

Notes

[a]A few states have negotiated with the U.S. Office of Education to use something other than "categories" for determining which children get services. These states are known as "noncategorical" states. Because only a few states have taken this route, the subtleties of noncategorical states are not considered here.

[b]Reputedly it was Goethe who said, "Tell me what you are looking for and I'll tell you what you will find." Clinical experience is the epitome of this maxim, and it should be regarded with skepticism. Certainly many 10-year-old children are still at the sensory-motor stage. We have not done any experiments to determine that more children with oppositional and defiant behaviors are stuck at the sensory-motor stage than are other children of similar age and mental ability.

7

Training
for Parents

At best, educators can use behavior engineering and applied behavior analysis techniques to manage the behavior of oppositional children during the school day. However, not a single study purports that teachers, acting alone, can effect broad-based behavior change in these children. The arena for achieving any fundamental, what might be called *systemic*, behavior change, is the home. When educators identify children who are markedly oppositional, they will want parents to participate in parent training. Some parent-training models are more effective than others. To make good referrals and to make them convincingly, educators need to know what constitutes good parent training. Educators also want to understand the techniques that the parents are learning so that, when the child is ready, the teachers can use similar techniques in the classroom and thereby make it more likely that the child will display the newly acquired behavior-control skills at school.

🔑 Key Concept

Behavior Parent Training has proven to be the most successful treatment for changing the child's noncompliant behaviors.

Behavior Parent Training (BPT)

Not surprisingly, the development of parent-training programs has a long history, as does the research into their effectiveness. In 1969, Hanf reported on a treatment protocol that he developed for training parents to modify their own behavior in order to increase their child's compliance.[1] The training consisted of instruction in the principles of operant conditioning and its application to child rearing, modeling the operant conditioning principles for the parents, and having the parents role-play the implementation of these skills. Retrospectively, this approach has been called Behavior Parent Training (BPT). In comparison with other approaches,[2] BPT has proven to be the most successful treatment for changing the behavior of children with conduct problems.

Patterson further developed BPT.[3,4] His Coercive Hypothesis expressed his belief that most parents unwittingly reinforce their child's aggression. Thus the central theme of his treatment program became teaching parents how to change the reinforcement contingencies. His treatment program required parents to read materials that described the basic concepts of operant conditioning techniques and how those principles applied to child rearing; to attend group therapy sessions in which the parents were guided by a therapist on how to use reinforcers to strengthen the child's prosocial behaviors; and then to develop a strategy designed to modify one or two of the child's aggressive behaviors by using such punishment techniques as point loss, time-out, or work details. Coming at the heyday of psychotherapy, Patterson's systematic and successful application of BPT was revolutionary.

Five Essential Parenting Skills

Forehand and McMahon further refined BPT by identifying five essential parenting skills.[5] They instructed the parents in these skills, had the parents role-play each skill, and then asked the parents to implement the skill during simulation sessions that involved the child picking up toys. While the parent successively implemented each skill in the simulation sessions, a therapist observed from behind a one-way mirror and coached via a microphone in the parent's ear. The parents were required to reach criteria on each skill, and assignments were given to generalize the use of the skills to the home. The five skills taught by Forehand and McMahon and subsequently used by all successful parent-training programs are (1) giving attends, (2) positive social reinforcement (praise), (3) ignoring, (4) giving alpha commands, and (5) compliance training and time-out.

Giving Attends. Attends are commentaries on the child's behavior, and they are employed to provide the child with a source of attention. Attends describe the child's behavior (e.g., "You're putting a puzzle together") or emphasize desired behavior (e.g., "You're reading a book"). Giving attends, which could also be called labeling, means using objective, nonvalue-laden terms to describe what a child is doing.

Attends have definite characteristics in terms of what they should and should not do. They should

- Be specific and descriptive;
- Describe actions in objective, nonjudgmental terms; and
- Let the child know that the parent is attending.

On the other hand, attends should not

- Make demands upon the child or
- Reinforce the child.

Correctly given, attends provide positive attention to the child and promote appropriate behavior.

Positive Social Reinforcement (Praise). Positive social reinforcement employs three types of rewards: physical rewards, unlabeled verbal rewards, and labeled verbal rewards. Physical rewards include assorted types of physical affection, such as hugs, kisses, and pats on the back. Unlabeled verbal rewards are nonspecific praise statements, such as, "Good job," "I like that," and "Nice work." Labeled verbal rewards are praise statements that describe the particular behavior the parent wishes to reinforce, such as "Thank you for putting your coat away," or "Thank you for helping me with the trash."

Praise describes what a child is doing and lets the child know that the parent values the behavior. It must be genuine and provided appropriately. Like attends, praise, in the context of BPT, has certain characteristics:

- Specific, descriptive, and valuing
- Nonintrusive and nondirective
- Reinforcing of the child's behavior
- Positively attentive to the child
- Promoting of appropriate behavior

Ignoring. In Forehand and McMahon's training model, it is vital for the parents to ignore their child's inappropriate behavior. The components of effective ignoring are the elimination of eye contact, nonverbal attention, verbal contact, and physical contact if the child is behaving inappropriately. Assuming that the parent's attention is a reinforcer, while the child is engaging in inappropriate behavior, that reinforcer is removed. Thus, ignoring as practiced by Forehand and McMahon is a time-out procedure and a mild punishment.

Giving Alpha Commands. Forehand and McMahon's model includes two types of commands: alpha commands and beta commands. Alpha commands are clear, concise commands. Beta commands are any directives that are not clear and concise. Any command that is not behaviorally specific (e.g., "Act your age!") is a beta command. A chain of commands (e.g., "Turn off the TV, pick up the toys, brush your teeth, and get to bed.") is a beta command. Requests that come in the form of a question (e.g., "Would you like to put your pajamas on now?") and "let's" commands (e.g., "Let's clean your room now.") are beta commands. Commands that are accompanied by a rationale or other verbalizations (e.g., "Clean up your room. It is messy and I want the house clean when your dad comes home.") are also beta commands.

Forehand and McMahon trained parents to recognize and avoid beta commands and to issue only alpha commands. Alpha commands, which are always requests for positive behavior, have the following characteristics. They

- Are specific and direct;
- Are given one at a time;
- Direct attention to positive behavior;
- Provide the child with an opportunity to act appropriately; and
- Allow the parent to reinforce appropriate positive behaviors.

It is important to reemphasize that alpha commands are requests for positive behavior. A "stop doing that" command is not an alpha command. If a 5-year-old was banging her spoon against the table, Forehand and McMahon would advise the parent against saying to the child, "Brenda, stop banging your spoon!" Presumably, they would suggest that the parent give Brenda an alpha command (i.e., a request for a positive behavior) that is incompatible with banging the spoon. For example, the parent might say, "Brenda, put your supper dishes in the sink." Brenda cannot keep beating her spoon against the table and also comply with the alpha command to put her dishes in the sink.

Compliance Training and Time-Out. In Forehand and McMahon's parent-training model, compliance is achieved through the use of time-out (TO). When given an alpha command, the child has five seconds to initiate compliance. After five seconds the command is repeated with a warning that either he complies or he will go to a time-out area. If the child fails to comply after an additional five seconds, the child is taken to the time-out area and told, "Since you didn't _____, you have to stay here until I say you can leave." Arguing and rationalizing are strongly discouraged. Also, the parent ignores tantrums, shouts, protests, or promises to behave. The time-out session lasts three minutes, and during the last 15 seconds of the session the child has to be sitting quietly on the chair. When the child is released from time-out, the parent repeats the original command. If the child again refuses to comply with the request, the entire sequence starts over.

The compliance training procedure is initially explained to the child, and the child verbalizes his understanding. Nonetheless, some children actively resist going to the time-out area and staying there. When this happens, Forehand and McMahon instruct the parents to spank the child. However, they caution that spanking can become an emotional release for the parent, and if the child becomes defiant and aggressive, which they often do, the spanking can become abusive.

We support all of the parenting techniques advocated by Forehand and McMahon except one: compliance training and time-out. Time-out is punishment, and punishing a child strains, if not breaks, the parent-child bond. Furthermore, if the child does not accept going to a time-out, the parent is told to spank the child. As described later, there are other approaches that can be used in lieu of compliance training and time-out.

  Key Concept

Four essential skills for successful parenting:

   1. Labeling the child's behavior.
   2. Praising the child.
   3. Ignoring inappropriate behavior.
   4. Making requests for positive behavior (giving alpha commands).

BPT Via Videotape

Carol Webster-Stratton, a productive and active researcher in the area of BPT and the risk factors for the development of children with conduct problems, developed videotapes that show people modeling the essential parenting skills.[6] To determine the effectiveness of videotape-based training, she conducted a study in which parents were divided into four groups. The parents in group one individually observed the videotapes of the essential parenting skills; the parents in group two jointly viewed the videotapes and discussed the material among themselves; the parents in group three had the material presented by a therapist and then discussed it, which is conventional BPT; and the parents in group four constituted a waiting-list control group. The follow-up data, which included observations of the child's behavior during home visits, indicated that the children of the parents in all three treatment groups exhibited significant behavior changes in comparison with the waiting-list control group, and that no particular treatment group was markedly superior to another.[7] This finding is significant because it suggests that videotapes might be a low-cost way to deliver effective BPT to a broad audience of parents such that, through the use of modern technology, anyone in any place and at any time can learn effective ways to mitigate a child's conduct problems.

Parent Training in Our University-Based Clinic

Initially, we worked directly with schools in our region to help them better serve children with oppositional and defiant behaviors. However, psychologists and counselors with the regional mental health center, physicians, and pediatric psychiatrists started to refer oppositional children to "our clinic." In response, we started one. The clinic served two purposes. The hands-on experience with oppositional children was great training for the graduate students in the school psychology program. In addition, we quickly realized that if the children were going to make long-term behavior changes, their parents needed to learn new skills and to be well integrated into the school's multidisciplinary, problem-solving team.

Composition of the Groups

After experience with groups composed of both of a child's parents and groups composed of mothers only, we concluded that the groups with the most cohesion, the least attrition, and the most substantive sharing were the mothers-only groups. Moreover, the children in the mothers-only group showed the most improvement in their behavior.

This conclusion that the mothers-only groups functioned the best was certainly influenced by the demographics of the parents seeking treatment. Consistent with the risk factors for children to develop oppositional behaviors, roughly 30 percent of the mothers referred for treatment were single. Mixing unmarried women with married women and their spouses created an unproductive and, at times, uncomfortable dynamic.

Philosophy

Our university-based clinic for children with oppositional and defiant behaviors and their mothers closely follows the Behavior Parent Training model pioneered by Patterson and refined by Forehand and McMahon. However, there are some subtle but fundamental differences.

When a child is noncompliant or demonstrates other inappropriate behavior, both Patterson and Forehand recommend that the parent punish the child. We do not believe in punishing children.[8] As Patterson points out, "The price for using an aversive to control behavior is that they will be returned in amount and perhaps in kind."[9] We concur, and we also believe the same could be said about any type of punishment. There is something about being punished that elicits in children a strong desire and often a well-laid plan to "get even." We have yet to meet the child who was punished and then, after several days of reflection, said, "Thanks. I needed that." Punishment is also undesirable because when parents resort to punishment they are being powerful models for the utility of aggression. It is hard to explain to children why an adult can use aggression to control someone's behavior, but they cannot. Finally, punishment does nothing to address the underlying cause of the child's behavior; punishment only temporarily suppresses the symptom, which often turns out to be a skill deficit—and once the skill deficit is addressed the inappropriate behavior disappears. Parents and teachers punish children for two reasons. First, it feels good. There is an emotional catharsis that comes from punishing a child who "really had it coming." In addition, adults punish children because, in the short term, punishment is effective. As long as the person who punished the child is present, the child is less likely to engage in the inappropriate behavior.

 Key Concept

Parents must learn how to manage a child's inappropriate behavior without resorting to punishment.

We are also opposed to punishing children for philosophical reasons. Punishment seems to be predicated on the premise that the goal of parenting is to control the child's behavior. We think that parenting is about establishing, over time, an equitable relationship with the child so that, by modeling, the child learns how to develop healthy relationships with others. Brofenbrenner elegantly expressed the goal, the process, and the complexity of parenting when he wrote that "learning and development are facilitated by the participation of the developing person in progressively more complex patterns of reciprocal activity with someone with whom that person develops a strong and enduring emotional attachment and when the balance of power gradually shifts in favor of the developing person."[10]

However, a position of no punishment begs an important question: What is a parent to do when the child behaves inappropriately? In lieu of punishment, we teach parents two skills and two concepts. The first skill is to ignore the behavior but not the child, and the second skill is to ignore and redirect. The two concepts are gentle interventions[11] and logical consequences.[12] This instruction and skill-building practice is done in eight group sessions that last about two hours each; in addition, every mother and child is asked to participate in seven private one-hour clinic sessions.

Our group training is based heavily on Forehand and McMahon's model and incorporates videotape modeling similar to Webster-Stratton's work. However, there are some differences.

Group Session 1—Introductions and Overviews

Coffee, soft drinks, and cookies are provided, and time is allotted for the participants to mingle while introductions are quietly facilitated. A brief overview of the training sessions is given, with particular emphasis on the expectations of the participants. Then the therapist tells the mothers about the three factors that put a child at risk for developing oppositional behaviors. The first risk factor addressed is parent stress. As part of the intake process, the mothers were asked to complete several questionnaires, including the Parenting Stress Index.[13] At this time, the therapist explains the instrument and asks each parent to examine her results. The mothers have an opportunity to share with the group their level of stress and some of the underlying contributors.

The therapist then gives an overview of the second risk factor for a child to develop oppositional behaviors—a difficult temperament. Again, the therapist asks each mother to talk about her child's temperament and to share whether she thinks that her child has an inherently difficult temperament. Almost without exception, they do. This sharing seems to give the mothers permission to tell their stories. They readily discuss their child's oppositional behavior and talk about the stress it has created in the family. Without exception, the mothers report their disenfranchisement from their immediate community. Some mothers feel alienated from their spouses, devalued by their in-laws and even by their parents. They feel that day care, preschool, and the public school have labeled them "poor parents." The sharing develops the cohesion of the group by making it clear that every mother is under considerable stress, is feeling isolated, and is at her wits' end with regard to changing her child's noncompliant behavior. The meeting concludes with each mother sharing her expectations for the training. It is mentioned that the program will provide the coffee and soft drinks for every meeting but that a volunteer is needed to bring cookies or some dessert to the next session. Being able to contribute to the group seems to further build commitment and cohesion.

Group Session 2—Labeling and Praising

Usually a few mothers come early to socialize a little before the group training starts. When the group training begins, the therapist discusses the third risk factor—parenting skills. The mothers are told that if they were raising a "normal" child, their current level of parenting skills would be just fine. However, parenting a child who inherently has a difficult temperament makes exceptional demands on parents. When raising such a child, one needs exceptionally good parenting skills, and the purpose of the training is to help them become super parents.

The therapist then explains the skill of "labeling," or, as Forehand and McMahon call it, "attends." A video of a mother modeling how to label is shown, and then, working in pairs, each mother role-plays the implementation of the skill while the other mother pretends to be the child. In a similar manner, the skill of praising is explained, and individual sessions are then scheduled in the clinic so both skills can be modeled and the mother can have guided practice acquiring them.

As a homework assignment, each mother is asked to do one activity with her child for roughly 10 minutes each evening. The activity is to be scheduled in advance with the child, and, if feasible, it is to be at the same time each evening. In addition, the activity must not make demands on the child. It is the child's time. The activity should have no right or wrong answers, and there should not, even by implication, be a winner and a loser. Finally, the activity cannot be passive, such as watching a TV show together. Commonly selected activities are reading a book to the child at bedtime, putting together a puzzle, dressing a doll, and building with Legos. During this activity, the mother is expected to practice the skills of labeling and praising and, immediately after each activity, to make a few notes about how the interaction went.

Finally, the mothers are given a daily log (see Figure 7.1) and instructed to begin completing it for the rows labeled Attend, Praise, and Engage. (Engage means the mother devotes at least 15 minutes that day engaging with the child in an activity of her interest.) As new

Figure 7.1
Parent's Daily Log

Mother's name _____

From _____ (date) _____ to _____ (date)

	Sunday	Monday	Tuesday	Wednesday	Thursday	Friday	Saturday
Attend							
Praise							
Engage							
Ignore							
Ignore & redirect							

Gently intervene	Natural consequence	Logical consequence	No punishment	Not give in to demands	Don't banter	Avoid "no"	No ultimatums

skills are taught each week, they complete the appropriate rows by putting a *yes* or a *no* in the appropriate boxes each day.

Group Session 3—Requesting Positive Behavior and Ignoring

Increasingly, more mothers come early to socialize and partake of the treats. When the session formally starts, the mothers share their experiences with the last week's assignment. Then the therapist explains the skill of requesting positive behavior (alpha commands and beta commands), and shows the participants a videotape of a mother modeling the skill with her child. Working in randomly determined pairs, each parent role-plays implementing the skill.

The therapist then introduces the skill of ignoring. Working in different pairs, each mother lists the behaviors that her child predictably displays that are bothersome or unacceptable. Each mother then shares her list with the group, and, during the sharing, other mothers add to their list. The mothers, working as a group and looking at all of the listed behaviors, put the behaviors into two categories. One category is the behaviors that threaten anyone's health and safety, portend property destruction, or impose on anyone's basic rights.[a] The second category is the child's behaviors that are irritating and that one wishes the child would not display, but that do not threaten health and safety, portend property destruction, or impose on anyone's basic rights. Through guided discussion, the mothers come to realize that the behaviors in the second category can and should be ignored. For example, one mother's daughter preferred to go to school with her hair in a ponytail, but the mother insisted that her daughter looked better in braids. Nearly every morning the mother and daughter had a battle royal over this issue. Another mother's daughter refused to eat certain foods that her parents deemed were good for her, and family meals often degenerated into a heated dispute about whether the girl was going to eat certain vegetables. But since when has not eating peas endangered a child's health? This classification activity gives the parents insight about when it is necessary to intervene and when certain behaviors should just be ignored. The lively discussion also empowers the mothers to take an active role in their own training.

The therapist explains to the mothers that ignoring a behavior means giving no indication whatsoever that they are aware of the behavior. A videotape of a mother modeling how to ignore inappropriate behaviors is shown. Then, working in randomly determined pairs, one mother acts out a particular inappropriate behavior from the other mother's list while the second mother practices ignoring the behavior. For a homework assignment, the mothers determine three behaviors they will ignore, and they are asked to note the effects of ignoring the behavior in their daily diary.

Later in the week, each mother and her child come to the clinic. If the mother has reached certain criteria in the skills of labeling and giving praise, the therapist demonstrates the skill of ignoring inappropriate behaviors while working with the child and then gives the mother an opportunity to practice the skill. This practice session is videotaped. Most mothers are surprised to find that ignoring—truly ignoring—their child's inappropriate behaviors is difficult. Although the mother does not verbally comment on her child's inappropriate behavior, she might as well. Her nonverbal behaviors scream out her disapproval. For example, when the child pushes a puzzle piece off the table, some mothers visibly move back several inches to put distance between themselves and the child. Others wrinkle their brow or frown. Another mother's voice takes on a slightly agitated tone, and nearly all mothers hesitate a moment before continuing to interact with their child. All of these nonverbal actions communicate the parent's disapproval. And with almost 100 percent predictability, a nonverbal act from the parent that communicates disapproval inflames the child, who often responds with noncompliance, defiance, and sometimes aggression.

As a homework assignment, each mother is asked to review her video and to write down the words, gestures, and nonverbal actions that she made every time she saw a behavior that she considered inappropriate. She also notes (i.e., scripts) whether she did anything to communicate her disapproval. With practice, which sometimes requires up to three sessions, each mother masters the skill of ignoring.

Group Session 4—Ignore and Redirect

After sharing the results of the two homework assignments (ignoring three behaviors and scripting the video of their clinic work), the mothers are taught the skill of requesting positive behavior following the now well-established process of instruction, watching a videotape of the skill being modeled, and dividing into pairs to role-play. Intentionally, no homework assignment is given at this time regarding this skill.

Next, the therapist introduces and teaches the skill of ignore and redirect. Ignore and redirect is necessary when the child's behavior threatens anyone's health or safety, portends property destruction, or imposes on other people's basic rights. For example, Ricky, a 4-year-old who was playing in a sandbox, started to throw sand at another child. Seeing this, his mother came to the door and called out, "Children, it's time to come in for some lemonade." At first blush, this seems like a coddling response to a child's aggression. However, the mother is not explicitly accepting the aggression. Rather, realizing that this is not a teachable moment, she is making the minimal intervention necessary to redirect Ricky away from behavior that could hurt someone. Being a good mother, at a later time she will give Ricky guidance and instruction so that he will not throw sand at his playmates.

Like the other parenting skills, ignore and redirect has certain important characteristics:

- Does not attend to inappropriate behaviors;
- Gently interrupts potentially harmful behaviors;
- Usually involves making an alpha command for an appropriate behavior; and
- Typically gives the caregiver an opportunity to praise the child.

The mothers leave with an assignment to use the ignore and redirect skill at least three times that week with the child.

Before the next group session, each parent comes to the clinic and watches the therapist model the skill of ignoring and redirecting with her child. Then the mother enters the clinic room and practices the skill of ignoring and redirecting with the child. Again, a videotape is made for self-study. Experience has shown that when mothers use ignore and redirect, they effectively respond to roughly 85 percent of a child's behaviors that threaten someone's health and safety, portend property destruction, or impose on someone's basic rights. Obviously, this one technique deals effectively with a great number of the child's problematic behaviors.

Finally, the therapist introduces and discusses the issue of age-appropriate expectations because, based on experience, many parents of children with oppositional and defiant behaviors have excessively high expectations for their child's level of independence, self-help skills, and social abilities. Targeting the ages represented by the children in each particular group, the mothers are given guidelines for the age-appropriate expectations in these three areas.

Group Session 5—Gentle Interventions

Occasionally, the ignore and redirect technique is not appropriate to the situation or does not work. When that happens, the parent is still obligated to do something to protect people and property and to restore the basic rights of others. Yet, even at those times it is essential to remember that *the goal of the intervention is to do only what is necessary to terminate unacceptable behavior*. For example, if Justin just hit another playmate, there is, at that moment, only one meaningful goal: to make the least intrusive intervention that ensures that Justin does not hit the playmate again. Realistically, it will not help if Mrs. Jensen opens the door and, in a loud authoritative voice, yells, "Justin, don't you dare hit Joey again." Instead, what is called for is a calmly administered gentle intervention. A gentle intervention is anything that the parent does, with the exception of punishment or bribery, that gets the child to immediately discontinue the behavior.

Gentle interventions exist on a continuum. The group is asked to develop a plausible continuum of gentle interventions from least intrusive to most intrusive. Most lists look something like the following:

- Come into the child's area of vision by being physically present.

- Make eye contact.

- Move closer to the child.

- Make a gesture such as waving a hand back and forth in a way that says "Cool it."

- Move between the child and the child's target, be it animate or inanimate.

- Make a verbal request for a positive behavior (i.e., an alpha command).

- Use a physical prompt such as putting a hand on the child's arm.

- Use physical restraint such as a basket hold.

The mothers are asked to refer back to their list of the child's inappropriate behaviors that cannot be ignored and to match each behavior with a response on the intervention continuum that probably would be sufficient to interrupt the behavior. For example, under "presence" (i.e., being physically present) one mother listed the following: putting underwear in the toilet, painting on the bathroom mirror with toothpaste, and pulling the cat's tail. In other words, if the mother catches the child engaging in any of those behaviors, she does not need to do or say anything to get the behavior terminated. Her presence is sufficient. When each mother is mentally equipped with her intervention continuum, she is prepared to interrupt the behavior with the least intrusive intervention.

There are two reasons to always start with the least intrusive intervention that seems likely to interrupt the behavior. First, children typically respond better, meaning they are more likely to discontinue the behavior, if the intervention does not threaten their dignity. Second, the increasingly intrusive intervention continuum has a corresponding behavior escalation continuum. It almost seems to be a law of nature that when animals, including children, resist an outside intrusion, they resist at the next highest level. For example, a mother walks into a room and finds her 4-year-old son coloring on the wall, so she gives him "the look." If the boy is going to resist Mom's intervention, the most likely thing he will do is look away and keep coloring on the wall. However, if she had grabbed him by the scruff of his neck and pulled him to his feet and he was determined to resist, he would have hit or kicked her.

Again, it should be stressed that a behavior that threatens people's health or safety, portends property destruction, or imposes on basic rights is not acceptable, and, if it persists, the behavior needs to be addressed. But at the moment the behavior is occurring, the major goal is to get the behavior stopped in an efficient, nonemotional, and effective manner. Proactive approaches for changing behaviors are discussed in Chapter 9.

Group Session 6—Natural Consequences and Logical Consequences

The parents are told that many of the child's decisions have natural consequences such that, without any intervention by an adult, a child's good decisions tend to lead to good outcomes and poor decisions tend to lead to poor outcomes. For example, if a child who lives in North Dakota decides not to put on a coat before going outside to play in January, he has made a poor decision, but it is no big deal. He will soon get cold, and when he gets cold he will come inside to get a coat.

Unfortunately, many parents intervene to protect the child from the natural consequence and, in doing so, bring about two poor outcomes. First, the intervening parent bears the brunt of the oppositional child's wrath. Second, the parent precludes the child from learning how to be a good decision maker or even from taking responsibility for his decisions. When this happens day after day, the long-term effects are a contentious parent-child relationship and a child who has not internalized a solid decision-making process.

Occasionally, the child makes a poor decision that does not have a sufficiently immediate natural consequence for the child to see the relationship between the decision and the outcome, or the natural consequence, if it were to happen, would be too severe. An example would be when a child refuses to confine her trike riding to the side-walk and insists on riding her trike in the street. The plausible natural consequence is getting run over by a car, and that natural consequence is too severe for any parent to accept. So the parent needs to invent a logical consequence.

A logical consequence is the relationship between how one behaves and what then happens as a result of those behaviors. Logical consequences can be positive, such as when responsible behavior leads to an increase in privileges, or logical consequences can be negative, such as when irresponsible behavior leads to loss of privileges to the extent necessary to protect health, safety, or basic rights.[12] This definition of logical consequences has three key components: (1) irresponsible behavior leads to a loss of privileges; (2) privileges are lost to the extent necessary to protect health, safety, or basic rights; and (3) a logical consequence is not punishment.

Going back to the girl who insists on riding her trike in the street, one parent response would be to spank the girl and then confine her to the house for an hour. Almost without exception, the child is going to resent that response. Another approach would be to think about what needs to happen so that she does not endanger herself. One logical consequence would be to explain to the girl the danger of riding the trike in the street and then to tell her that, to protect her from being run over by a car, the trike will be locked in the garage except at designated hours when someone (for example, an older sibling, mother, or father) is around to supervise.

Invariably, children understand and accept patiently explained logical consequences. It makes sense to them that they cannot do things that could hurt themselves or others; and, if they have behaviors or make decisions that could hurt themselves or others, it is necessary to reduce their privileges so that they and others are protected.

To learn how to develop logical consequences, the mothers again work in pairs. Each mother reviews the behaviors generated from the "ignore" assignment and from this list makes two subsets. One subset consists of the behaviors that have a natural but not excessively severe consequence sufficient to promote learning (for example, the behavior of the North Dakota boy who insists on going out to play in January without a coat). The other subset consists of the behaviors that are either so damaging that immediate action must be taken or for which there is not a sufficiently immediate natural consequence to promote learning. Each mother then shares subset one, the list slated for natural consequences, with the group. Then the mothers pair off to look at the behaviors in subset two (those behaviors that need a logical consequence) and they work together to determine a logical consequence for each of these behaviors. The mothers share one behavior and its planned logical consequence with the group, and the group gives the mother feedback as to whether her proposed action is really a logical consequence or thinly disguised punishment.

The mothers, along with many teachers or other caretakers, generally struggle with developing logical consequences. American culture is so heavily imbued with a punishment mentality that many caretakers have a difficult time seeing the difference between punishment and a logical consequence. It takes practice to develop logical consequences that do not inflict punishment and restrict privileges only to the extent necessary to protect people's health and safety, to safeguard property, and to ensure the basic rights of others.

Group Session 7—Routines

As previously mentioned, oppositional children do not respond well to being told what to do. Mothers report long, drawn-out conflicts getting their child to do daily tasks. Typically, the mother asks, coerces, harangues, and badgers the child to do the activity, and the child badgers and argues right back until, worn down, the parent either gives up or explodes in anger.

Routines are very useful for breaking up this destructive parent-child dynamic. To get started in using routines, each mother selects a time of day that is particularly difficult for her child and then develops a routine to implement during that time. One mother identified bedtime as the trouble spot. Her daughter, Emily, routinely delayed bedtime. She refused to quit watching television, to take her bath, or to brush her teeth.

As much as possible, the child should be involved in the task of developing a routine. With her mother's help, Emily developed the following routine:

7:00 Homework
7:30 Television
8:00 Clean up room
8:10 Games on the computer
8:30 Take a bath
8:55 Put on pajamas
9:00 Bedtime snack
9:15 Brush teeth
9:20 Reading time with Mom
9:35 Lights out

A successful routine has several keys. One key is to incorporate the Premack Principle.[14] The Premack Principle says that the opportunity to do a high-frequency behavior, such as watching television, can reinforce a low-frequency behavior, such as doing homework. It has also been called "Grandma's Rule"—you have to eat your peas before you get ice cream. So Emily's opportunity to play on the computer is made contingent on her cleaning up her room. If Emily does not clean up her room by 8:10, then she does not get to use the computer until the clean-up is complete. At 8:30, however, the time to use the computer expires. If Emily does not get her room clean until 8:35, then it is time, according to the schedule, to take a bath. Similarly, at the end of the routine, being read to by her mother is contingent on Emily's brushing her teeth.

Another key to a successful routine is using only reinforcers over which the parent has control. For example, using the opportunity to watch TV as a reinforcer for completing homework works only if the child accepts the parents' right to control the television. Similarly, a snack cannot be used to reinforce bathing and putting on pajamas if Emily will readily go to the kitchen and, despite her mother's directive, get what she wants to eat.

Involving the child is another key to a successful routine. For example, Emily and her mother discussed what activities should happen each evening, and they worked together to develop the sequence. When the routine was determined, Emily created a chart on the computer and ran off copies. Younger children can find magazine pictures that represent activities in the routine, such as brushing teeth, taking a bath, and eating a snack. The parent and child can then paste the pictures on the chart.

Charting each activity is another key to a successful routine. The child needs to check off each task on the chart as it is accomplished. This self-monitoring keeps the child focused on the desired behavior at each particular moment. Also, a checkmark on the chart gives the parent an opportunity to praise appropriate behavior. Finally, when the child gets off task, the charting process allows the parent to redirect the child without telling or ordering, and thus the chart avoids the "badgering" (i.e., a succession of compliance requests given with increased emotional intensity) that formerly was associated with getting the child to do daily tasks. For example, if it is computer time and Emily has not taken a bath, her mother only needs to ask, "Emily, what does your chart say?"

Another key to having a successful routine is foreshadowing, which was explained in Chapter 4. Most children get distracted and are not good time managers. Parents need to give the child reminders about upcoming changes and thus set the child up for success and not for failure. For example, Emily's mother might want to say, "Emily, computer time will be over in five minutes. If you get to the end of a game, you may not want to start another."

There is one final key to establishing a successful routine. Parents must prepare themselves for when the child does not do the necessary task and then throws a temper tantrum to get the reward. It is essential that if Emily does not get her homework done, she does not get to watch TV at 7:30. Parents can be sure that after about a week of successfully following the routine, their child will challenge the necessity of the chart. If the parents give in, they can forget about the chart being effective in the future.

Working in pairs, the mothers develop a plausible routine to have in mind when they sit down with their child, and they make sure they have carefully considered and appropriately spaced reinforcing activities. The homework assignment is to schedule a meeting with the child to develop a routine, to work with the child to write out the routine, and then to implement it.

⚷ *Key Concept*

The skills necessary to manage inappropriate behavior are the following:

- *Ignore the behavior, but not the child.*
- *Redirect.*
- *Make gentle interventions.*
- *Use logical consequences.*
- *Develop routines.*

Group Sessions 8 and 9—Individual Problem Solving

When the mothers have acquired the tools for responding to their child's oppositional behavior, they are invited to share any remaining problem areas and use the support of the group to develop plausible solutions. During this stage of the training, the mothers are actively encouraged to telephone each other for ideas and to come to the meeting with both a problematic issue and a proposed solution.

The value of the last two sessions cannot be overstated. The problem-solving process both asks and empowers parents to apply the skills they have learned to their own situation. The following examples represent three different types of problems commonly encountered by parents.

Case 1. Cody, age 8, and his mother fought every morning over his getting ready in time to catch the bus. The battle started first thing in the morning. Cody would not get out of bed. Mrs. Calliowitz literally had to pull Cody kicking and screaming out of bed. Once awake, he was no longer interested in sleeping, but he wanted to pop a video into the VCR and watch cartoons, which his mother allowed because it gave her time to get breakfast ready for him and the rest of the family. When breakfast was ready, Cody readily ate it. But after breakfast, he wanted to go back and finish watching his video. Mrs. Calliowitz brought Cody's clothes into the living room and struggled to dress him while he resisted. Then, if she was lucky, the cartoon ended, and she could get Cody to use the bathroom, wash, and brush his teeth. However, if the cartoon had not ended, she had to drag him into the bathroom and hold him while she washed him, brushed his teeth, and combed his hair. Finally, the bus could be seen and heard coming up the lane to the farmhouse. Invariably, Cody resisted getting on the bus, and his mother had to carry him out to the bus kicking and screaming.

Mrs. Calliowitz and Cody developed a routine that used video watching as a reinforcer for getting out of bed and getting dressed. Eating breakfast was used as a reinforcer for Cody to get washed, comb his hair, and brush his teeth. Then it was time for Cody to get on the bus. When they developed the routine, Mrs. Calliowitz had told Cody that it was his decision as to whether he was ready for the bus when it came and whether he got on the bus. If he did not get on the bus, the bus would wait for two minutes and then it would leave without him. If he missed the bus, he would stay at home on the farm that day.

Like most mothers, Mrs. Calliowitz was certain that her child couldn't care less whether he caught the bus and that the natural consequence would never work. However, when the routine was implemented, it never failed. Cody has now gone for three years without missing the bus.

Case 2. Brandon, age 5, had a tantrum every time his mother took him with her into a grocery store. Sometimes Brandon had a tantrum before they got to the end of the first aisle, and sometimes he did not throw a tantrum until they were in the checkout line; but he always had a tantrum. When a total stranger offered to give him a good spanking, it was the last straw for Mrs. Helms. Even though it would be a great inconvenience for her, she vowed to never again take Brandon grocery shopping.

From Brandon's perspective, while he was in the grocery store there were no clearly defined positive expectations. The only expectation was that he not throw a tantrum. If he behaved well for 15 minutes or even a half hour before he had a tantrum, he still failed. One parent suggested to Mrs. Helms that she apply the concept of a routine to the grocery store experience. Someone else pointed out that it would be useful to give Brandon tasks and then reward positive behavior. Before each shopping trip, Mrs. Helms could think of two things in each aisle that Brandon could find and safely put into the shopping cart (for instance, she wouldn't ask him to get things in glass jars or on high shelves). As the last thing purchased in the store, Brandon could select one item for the family, such as ice cream, from three choices.

Brandon's mother presented this idea to him, and together they planned their next trip to the grocery store. As part of the planning, Mom and Brandon thumbed through magazines to find pictures of the 10 items he was to find. They cut out the pictures and pasted them on a chart. Beside each picture was space for putting a checkmark. Mom then gave Brandon the choice of 3 possible things that he could buy after he had gathered the 10 items. As part of this planning, Mom told Brandon that if he insisted on getting another item before he found all 10 items on the chart, they would immediately leave the store. She reviewed the rules with him just before they went into the grocery store. The outing was successful. Follow-up a year later revealed that all subsequent "planned" grocery outings had gone smoothly. A couple of unplanned, last-minute trips to the grocery store had been disasters.

Case 3. Paul, age 5, followed his bedtime routine very well, but once he was in bed, he did not stay there. After a book was read and his mother kissed him good night, he would wait about five minutes and then get up and want to watch television with his parents or have another snack. If his demand was not met, he had a tantrum.

Paul's behavior presented a conundrum. It was inappropriate, and it evoked a strong desire to give him a good swat on the rear and put him back to bed. In truth, that would probably have worked. But, given the significant disadvantages of punishment, what is another solution?

One solution would be for Paul's mother to turn out the light and lay beside Paul for 15 minutes. In that time, he would probably go to sleep or at least get sufficiently drowsy to lose interest in getting out of bed. Paul's mother could make this even more effective by closing the heat register in his room so that his bed was warm and snug and the room was cool. However, Paul's mother didn't like this approach.

When faced with difficult situations, it is useful to go back to the fundamental concepts. One fundamental concept is the matter of when an intervention is necessary. We have stated that the behavior can be ignored if it does not threaten anyone's health or safety, portend property destruction, or impose on anyone's basic rights. When Paul gets out of bed, can that be ignored? By these criteria, the answer is yes. However, just because a behavior can be ignored does not mean that a parent should allow it to be reinforced. So when Paul gets out of bed at 9 o'clock, he should not be able to watch TV or get a snack. The family decided that it was possible to remove these reinforcers. Paul's mother likes to watch a certain TV show on Wednesday nights at 9 o'clock, and she has a small TV in her bedroom. She decided that she could go to her bedroom and lock the door. Paul's father, who always reads the evening newspaper, decided he could turn off the TV in the living room at 9 o'clock and read. The only remaining reinforcer to remove was the snack. Paul's parents decided they could easily put the snack foods out of Paul's reach.

The first evening that this strategy was in place Paul got out of bed after his mother turned off the light and left his room. He walked into the living room and tried to engage his dad, but his father ignored him. Paul went to the kitchen and looked for something to snack on, but he found nothing. He went to his mother's bedroom door and pounded on it, yelling to be let in. She did not respond. Paul went back to the living room and pushed the "on" button for the TV, but it did not start. His dad had unplugged it. Paul had a tantrum, but his dad ignored him. In short order, Paul crawled up on the sofa beside his dad and went to sleep. When his dad was ready to go to bed, he threw a blanket over Paul and left him asleep on the sofa. Sometime during the night, Paul woke up, walked into his room, and went to bed. That was the last time Paul got out of bed after 9 o'clock.

The Effectiveness of Behavior Parent Training

A recent review of the literature looked at 177 studies to determine the effectiveness of BPT.[15] Whereas most of the studies found evidence for the effectiveness of BPT, the success was determined only by looking at pre-treatment and post-treatment data without the benefit of comparing the treatment group against a control group that had no treatment. Many good things happen over the course of time, including children showing more responsible behavior. To make a valid claim that the treatment accounted for the children's improved behavior, the researchers needed to compare their gains against the gains of children in a no-treatment control group. Only 26 of 77 studies involving modification of children's antisocial behavior met the criterion of having a control group. A meta-analysis (a statistical approach that looks at the gain achieved as a result of the treatment) of these 26 studies concluded that the evidence indicates that BPT is effective in modifying children's behavior and enhancing parents' adjustment.

However, there are significant qualifiers. Sixty-six percent of the studies claiming that BPT is effective based their conclusion on evidence that the child's behavior was worse at the beginning of the treatment than it was at the end of the treatment. Some of the 26 studies that used a control group concluded that the treatment was successful because the parents reported improvements in their children's behavior. However, parents' assessments often are not supported by the observations of objective raters.[16] There is also the issue of "statistically significant" change in the child's behavior versus "clinically significant change." Some studies concluded that the treatment had a significant effect, statistically speaking, even though the child's behavior was still abnormal and basically unacceptable.[17] Finally, improvement in the child's behavior at home typically does not generalize to improvements at school or with peer relationships.[18]

Another shortcoming of BPT is that many parents do not complete the training, or, if they do, they become disengaged, as evidenced by missing many treatment sessions and not doing the homework assignments.[19] Some studies have reported dropout rates as high as 60 percent.[20] Unfortunately, it is the parents most at risk for raising a child with oppositional and defiant behaviors (e.g., lower socioeconomic status, unemployed, acute financial problems,[21] drug addiction,[22] single mothers,[23] and poor marital relations[24,25]) who are most likely to drop out of treatment and, if they do stay in treatment, have poor outcomes.[26] It turns out that parent training is likely to be successful only when the parent-child relationship is the major family problem.[27]

 Key Concept

Behavior Parent Training is most likely to be successful when the parent-child relationship is the only significant problem.

Several methodologically sound studies have examined the long-term effects of BPT on the children's behavior.[28,29] They found that one to two years after treatment, 30 to 40 percent of successfully treated parents reported their children were again having significant behavior problems. In short, Behavior Parent Training is the best treatment available; for many families it is not a panacea. Educators cannot simply identify children with oppositional behaviors, encourage their parents to receive behavior training, and wait for a compliant, well-behaved child to walk into their classroom.

Note

[a]The "endanger basic rights" criterion needs further amplification. For example, a parent has a right to expect to sleep undisturbed after a certain time at night, say 10 o'clock. If the child is up listening to music at full volume at 10:30 p.m., she is imposing on her father's basic right to get needed sleep. Is a 10-year-old child who pushes his peas around his plate with his finger during supper imposing on anyone's basic rights? No. It is poor table manners and indicates a skill deficit that must eventually be addressed, but if it is not a teachable moment, then the behavior can be ignored.

8

Treating the Child

Some children arrive in this world with temperaments that make it difficult for them to get along with others, and their innate temperament puts them at risk for developing oppositional behaviors.[1] Two approaches have been taken to directly help these children. One approach is prescribing medications that modify the child's temperament, and the other approach is equipping these children with the understandings that allow them to better control their behavior.

Pharmacological Treatment

If a child has an inflamed throat and an elevated temperature and a culture determines that the cause is streptococcus, a physician prescribes an antibiotic, probably streptomycin. The drug literally kills the offending bacteria and completely cures the disease. Children with oppositional behaviors also have symptoms (noncompliance, defiance, inattention, aggression, etc.), but there is no pill that brings about a cure. At best, a physician can prescribe medications that suppress the symptoms.

Aggression

Many children with oppositional and defiant behaviors are aggressive. A preponderance of evidence associates decreased levels of serotonin and of 5-hydroxyindole acetic acid (5-HIAA) with aggression (see Chapter 1).[2] Fortunately, a child's proclivity toward aggression can often be decreased by medications that increase the levels of serotonin,[3] such as Risperdal (risperidone), Seroquel (quetiapine), and Zyprexa (olanzapine), and also by pharmacological agents, such as lithium carbonate[4] and carbamazepine,[5] that increase 5-HIAA concentrations in the cerebrospinal fluid.

Impulse and Rage Control

From time to time, many oppositional children explode over an insignificant issue. It has been found that anticonvulsants such as Tegretol (carbamazepine) and Epival (divalproex) suppress the magnitude and the frequency of these outbursts.[6] Evidence indicates that Catapres (clonidine), a medication first used to treat hypertension, is also useful for children who have problems with impulse or rage control.[7]

Depression

Clinically depressed boys tend to become irritable, short-tempered, and aggressive, which are behaviors also commonly seen in oppositional children. Wellbutrin (bupropion), Tofranil (imipramine), Pamelor (nortriptyline), and other antidepressants that work well for adults seem to also work for clinically depressed children.[8]

Anxiety

The cardinal symptoms of anxiety include irritability and hypervigilance, which are again symptoms seen in many children with conduct problems. Tofranil (imipramine) and BuSpar (buspirone) have been suggested for the treatment of anxiety.[9]

Attention Deficit Hyperactivity Disorder (ADHD)

ADHD is often *comorbid* with oppositional behaviors—meaning they often occur together.[a] In the 1970s it was realized that Ritalin (methylphenidate hydrochloride), a stimulant, helped hyperactive children become more focused and less distracted and, when in school, remain more on task. It seemed so illogical that a stimulant could help overly active children slow down and focus that prescribing Ritalin was called a paradoxical treatment. Yet Ritalin became the medication of choice for treating ADHD for one simple reason: it worked.

Later, research caught up with practice, and it was discovered that hyperactive children have insufficient brain activity in their frontal lobes, the area of the brain that actively filters out irrelevant stimuli.[10] Ritalin enhances the ability of the frontal lobe to perform its executive functions.[11] Under the influence of Ritalin, children with ADHD can focus on weaker, but academically appropriate, stimuli so they can concentrate on their work and stay on task.

In addition to Ritalin, other commonly prescribed brand-name stimulants for ADHD are Adderall (amphetamine), Concerta (methylphenidate hydrochloride), Dexedrine (dextroamphetamine), and Metadate (methylphenidate hydrochloride). Cylert (magnesium pemoline) is a stimulant that also increases a child's ability to pay attention, but it is now infrequently used because of reports of liver failure in children using the drug.

Taken orally, Ritalin acts quickly. A child who swallows 10 milligrams of Ritalin at 8 o'clock in the morning is ready by 8:30 to attend to schoolwork. However, Ritalin in its conventional form is short acting. It is metabolized and out of the system within four hours. So the child typically takes a second pill at noon, which lasts for another four hours, or until it is time to go home at the end of the school day. Thus parents do not see the effects of Ritalin on the child, and they often erroneously conclude that the medication is not effective. Indeed, it is common for parents to say, "I can't see any difference." They probably can't. The medication didn't take effect until the child was in school, and it was out of the child's system by the time he got home.

Parents often do not see any effects of Ritalin for another reason. In the typical child with ADHD, the effects are apparent only when the child is required to sit still for long periods of time, listen intently, concentrate on schoolwork, and stay on task. This type of attending behavior is required hour after hour in school, but it is seldom required at home. At home, the ADHD child does not have any problems because she usually can flit from one interest to another and direct her own activities.

However, occasionally a child with ADHD will display new and significant behavior problems at home when placed on Ritalin. This increased agitation and aggressiveness at home are probably due to the "rebound effect." The rebound effect occurs when the body's natural *homeostatic process* (its efforts to return to the normal state) coincides with medication being metabolized out of the system. When this happens, the child experiences a considerable suppression of executive functions. If the child is then given expectations and demands, significant behavior problems will probably occur.

There are two final caveats about ADHD and Ritalin. As a group, educators tend to be too quick to suggest that a child has ADHD and to push parents to have the child placed on medication. Ritalin's effectiveness is partly to blame for this problem. When a child with ADHD is given Ritalin, it usually makes a world of difference in the classroom. Teachers who did not know how effective Ritalin could be often comment, "Why, you wouldn't believe it's the same kid!" It is hardly surprising that the teacher who sees how well Ritalin worked for Justin wonders whether Ritalin would also help Susie, the little girl who dawdles at her assignments. So the educator suggests to Susie's parents that she might have ADHD and could benefit from Ritalin.

Wanting to support the educator, Susie's parents make an appointment for Susie to be seen by their family physician or possibly Susie's pediatrician. Typically, the physician sees Susie in a medical examination room, interviews the parent, and through them, hears about the educator's observations and concerns. ADHD does not show up in a blood test, a urine analysis, a culture, or an X-ray. The diagnosis is made entirely on the basis of observed behaviors, and one of the poorest places to make such observations is the doctor's examination room. Given the benign side effects of Ritalin, most physicians are understandably willing to prescribe the medication and see if it makes a difference. However, again the physician is hindered by lack of information. Both the teacher and the child expect and want the Ritalin to make a difference, so they are not objective observers. Expecting to feel different, the child tries to pay better attention, and the teacher, expecting to see his prediction confirmed, pays particular attention to the times that Susie is on task. In short, the physician often has to base a decision about the medication's effectiveness, and ergo the validity of the diagnosis, on biased feedback.

 Key Concept

Before referring a child for possible medication, the education team should do a comprehensive evaluation of the child with an emphasis on the target behaviors.

A better approach, and one that parents should insist on, is to have the educational team prepare a comprehensive report for the examining physician. A school psychologist—one who has experience evaluating children for ADHD—should be a member of the team. The report should specify the child's presenting problem (target behaviors) in terms of observable behaviors and describe the circumstances under which these problematic behaviors typically occur. In the case of ADHD, the presenting problem could be in the area of completing schoolwork, paying attention during instructional time, behavior, or all of these. The report should contain information from the following sources.

The Child's Cumulative File. One diagnostic criterion for ADHD is that the disorder had to be present before age 7. That does not mean that the child has to be diagnosed with ADHD before age 7, but it does mean that, in retrospect, there was reason to believe that before age 7 the child had significant symptoms of ADHD. Almost invariably, the child's cumulative school records reveal traces of the symptoms.

An unmedicated child's report cards from kindergarten and 1st grade often show signs of ADHD. The evidence lies in the section of the report card in which the teacher rates the child in such areas as listening, work completion, following directions, and following rules. If there are problems in any of these areas, the teacher checks "N" for Needs Improvement, and such notations suggest that the child might have ADHD. Also, the school record will reveal if the child was retained in an early grade "due to immaturity," which can be another sign of ADHD. Another ADHD clue in the child's school file are "discipline" slips. At most schools, discipline slips are placed in the file when the child is sent to the principal's office.

The school record also contains scores on nationally normed achievement tests, which could either be additional evidence to suggest ADHD or might rule out ADHD as a reason for the child's attention problems. A downward trend in the scores on nationally normed achievement tests from grade to grade is a possible indicator of ADHD. This is because in kindergarten and 1st grade the children are paced from one test item to the next by the teacher's directions, and the educator makes sure the students pay attention and move together from item to item. Later, and certainly by the 4th grade, the children move through subtests at their own speed within an allotted time. At this point, the performance of a child with attention problems begins to slip. Also, a detailed analysis of test items will usually show more right answers at the beginning of each subtest than at the end of the subtest even though the items do not get progressively harder. The analysis might even show that the student did not complete many of the later items on the subtest. Another indicator of ADHD can be obtained by comparing the results of a nationally normed achievement test, in which the child's ability to pay attention is a factor, with an individually administered test. An unmedicated child with ADHD will generally do better on the individually administered achievement test because, again, an educator moves the child from item to item and manages the attention issues.

Sometimes the child's scores on the nationally normed achievement tests tend to rule out ADHD as a plausible explanation for problems with attention and work completion. This happens when, year after year, the child's achievement scores have been consistently low, which suggests the possibility that the child does not understand the material and lacks the ability to do many of the assignments.

Teacher Rating Form. A number of behavior checklists on the market are designed to be sensitive to the behaviors typically displayed by children who have ADHD. The Conners' Rating Scale is one of the better ones.[12] A thorough assessment includes having the classroom teacher, and possibly a parent, complete such a rating form. The best rating forms consist of some items that are consistent with attention problems and some items that "look" like they are indicative of children with ADHD but are not. Any form that has a title splashed across the top saying something such as "The Attention Deficit Rating Form" and that consists of only questions pertaining to ADHD-related behaviors is suspect. After all, the teacher referred Susie because he thinks she has ADHD. It would hardly be surprising that, when asked to complete an ADHD rating form, he gave Susie ratings that supported his supposition.

Peer Comparison. The school psychologist should make several classroom observations of Susie. The observations should occur when Susie needs to be paying attention to the teacher's instructions and also at times when she needs to be working independently. During these observations, Susie's off-task behaviors should be compared with the off-task behaviors of another "typical" child of the same gender in the same classroom. Time sampling at set intervals is a good way to collect the data. In this method, the school psychologist looks up every 15 seconds and takes a mental picture of what Susie is doing at that instant and also of what her comparison peer is doing, and he records this information on a chart like the one shown in Figure 8.1. The school psychologist notes whether Susie, at that instant of observation, is verbally off task (talking), motor off task (e.g., spinning a pencil), passive off task (staring into space or looking around), or out of her seat. The observer collects the same data at the same instance for the comparison peer. By doing a Sign Test, the school psychologist can compute whether Susie really is off task more than the "typical" child in the classroom.[b] Each such classroom observation can be done in five minutes, and at least four such observations should be made at various times and during various activities over the course of a week.

Figure 8.1
Classroom Observation Form

Classroom Observation

Date: _____

Observer: _____

School: _____

Teacher: _____

Grade: _____

Age (Child #1): _____

Age (Child #2): _____

Activity: _____

Time Begun: _____

Time Stopped: _____

Total Time: _____

15-Second Intervals

Behavior	Child	15	30	45	60	15	30	45	60	15	30	45	60	15	30	45	60	15	30	45	60
Verbal Off Task	1																				
	2																				
Motor Off Task	1																				
	2																				
Passive Off Task	1																				
	2																				
On Task	1																				
	2																				
Out of Seat (Duration)	1																				
	2																				

For some children with ADHD, the major problem is their behavior, such as impulsive acts and remarks, interrupting the teacher, and minor but annoying aggression toward peers (poking people in the ribs, thumping students on the arms, etc.). In such cases, the school psychologist should do sufficient observations to determine the frequency, context, and function of these behaviors.

Functional Behavior Assessment. The school psychologist should also complete a functional behavior assessment. A functional behavior assessment simply means that someone skilled at observing behavior tries to determine the function (i.e., the reason) for the child's behavior. A functional behavior assessment provides plausible answers to two related questions: What is causing Susie to get off task? What benefits is Susie deriving from her off-task behavior?

A functional behavior assessment is completed by observing the child in the classroom and noting each incident of the target behavior, which, in Susie's case, is her off-task behavior. The observer notes and records what happened just before each target behavior (i.e., the antecedent), and also what happened right after the target behavior (i.e., the consequence). If the school psychologist can start to predict when Susie is going to be off task, then perhaps she does not have ADHD. For example, if Susie is off task whenever she has to read independently, then ADHD is probably not the reason. More likely, she is a poor reader or possibly she has a vision problem.[c] If Susie is off task because she is whispering to a classmate, then, again, ADHD probably is not the problem. She likely has a strong social need for acceptance and validation, and fulfilling this need takes precedence over her need to acquire information.

A functional behavior assessment is important because there are many reasons why children have problems paying attention, and ADHD is just one of them. Some additional reasons are depression, anxiety, hearing problems, vision problems, inability to do the schoolwork, a central auditory processing disorder, or the teacher's difficulties in managing the classroom. A functional behavior assessment seldom confirms that any one of these culprits is guilty of causing the child's attention problems, but it can uncover clues that merit further investigation.

Computer Testing. Two commonly used computer-generated assessments of a child's attention abilities are the Test of Variables of Attention (TOVA)[13] and the Conners' Continuous Performance Test (CPT).[14] The CPT requires the child to look at letters being flashed one at a time on a computer screen. The child is told, "Push the space bar each time a letter is flashed. Push the space bar after seeing each letter, except for X. Do not push the space bar when an X flashes." The test lasts 15 minutes, and when it is over, a report is printed that compares the child's response pattern with that of similar-aged, same-gender peers and gives a probability statement about whether the child's response pattern is consistent with ADHD. The TOVA is similar to the CPT except that, in its newest version, the TOVA has supplemented the visual-attending task with an auditory-attending task.

A computer-generated test of attention is a nice objective assessment. However, it should not be regarded as the final word about whether Susie should be given medication for ADHD. Some unmedicated students with ADHD do just fine in well-organized, highly structured classrooms.

Attempted Accommodations. Many children who have mild ADHD can be successfully served in the classroom if they are provided with a few minor modifications. For example, Susie might be able to complete her deskwork assignments if, during these times, she sat at a study carrel that reduced her visual distractions. Justin might sit still and listen if, at those times, he had a ball of clay to roll and squeeze and keep his hands busy. Jason might stop bothering other students if a square of red tape was placed on the floor around his desk to remind him to stay in his area. Such minor modifications often sufficiently mitigate the presenting problem and eliminate the need to put the child on medication. Before referring the child for medications, some such accommodations should be attempted.

⚷ Key Concept

A referral for possible medication should include a written report that contains data on the target behaviors.

Written Report. The school psychologist should collect all of this information, summarize it in a written report, and share the findings with the referring teacher and the parents. If the team feels that the data are consistent with ADHD, that other plausible reasons for Susie's slowness in completing work assignments have been ruled out, and that appropriate classroom accommodations have been tried, a referral should be made to a physician.

Monitoring. About one-third of the children who have ADHD do not benefit from the prescribed medication.[15] Either the level of the dose needs to be adjusted to fit the child's metabolism, or the child should stop taking the medication because, as sometimes happens, that particular medication is ineffective. Ideally, monitoring the efficacy of stimulant medications is done over four weeks, using four drug regimens, and neither the raters of the child's behavior (i.e., the school psychologist, the teacher, and possibly the parent) nor the child know which regimen was taken on any day. The four drug regimens are a light dose of stimulant, a moderate dose, a high dose, and a placebo. At the end of the month, the data are matched against the actual regimen used and the efficacy of each drug condition is determined.[16]

The school psychologist should take the lead role in designing and collecting the necessary data to determine whether the medication has improved Susie's ability to complete her work assignments. The collected information should be quantified. This tends to ensure that the target behavior is observable and objective and can be easily conveyed via a summary chart. For example, if "difficulty completing written assignments" is a target behavior, a daily log showing the number of work assignments completed (in the numerator) and the number of deskwork assignments given (in the denominator) coupled with a percentage-of-work-completed graph would provide good, objective data for determining the efficacy of the medication. The data would be particularly useful if they were collected about a week before the medication was initiated to determine a baseline. Each time Susie sees her physician, the most recent copy of the data should accompany her. Of course, a similar report should accompany any child who is referred to a family physician, a child psychiatrist, or a pediatrician for possible psychopharmacology medications.

Training for School-Aged Children

In clinic settings, the behavior of children with conduct disorders, including those with oppositional behavior, has been successfully changed following child-training therapy.[17-21] These successful child-training programs are based on the model developed by Kendall and Braswell.[22] They describe their approach as social-cognitive problem solving.[d]

In Kendall and Braswell's opinion, children's conduct problems typically occur because they have ineffective techniques for solving problems, and many of their conduct problems would lessen if they had better problem-solving skills. Specifically, these children need to recognize and admit the problem, reflect on possible solutions, make a decision, and take action. Because their main problems center on relationships, these children need particular help in learning to solve social problems. Kendall and Braswell's approach to child training consists of several steps.

Self-instruction. The child is taught the following rubric for problem solving:

- Problem definition: "Let's see, what am I supposed to do?"
- Problem approach: "I have to look at all of the possibilities."
- Focusing attention: "I'd better concentrate and focus."
- Self-reinforcement: "Hey, good work!"
- Coping statement: "Oh, I made a mistake. Next time I'll. . . ."

Initially, the therapist models this self-instruction rubric; then she guides the child through it many times using a wide variety of problems. The goal is that the child internalizes the self-instructional rubric and eventually applies it to real-life situations.

Self-reward. When the child effectively follows the rubric, he should congratulate himself (e.g., "Wow! I really concentrated on that"). Initially, the therapist nurtures the development of this self-reward mechanism by richly praising good efforts (e.g., she tells the child, "You are really trying hard"). Kendall and Braswell take pains to point out that the child is rewarded for his effort and not for getting the correct solution (i.e., the therapist does not say, "Good going! You got the right answer").

Response Cost. At the start of the training, the therapist gives the child a number of tokens and tells him that he can earn more tokens, but he can also lose tokens. He loses tokens by making a mistake on task instructions, getting a wrong answer, forgetting a step of the self-instruction rubric, or going too fast. Kendall and Braswell believe taking away tokens curbs impulsive answers and trains the child to think before acting.

Self-evaluation. The child is asked to complete the self-evaluation scale (Figure 8.2) regarding use of the problem-solving rubric. After the first session, the therapist completes the rating while explaining her rationale to the child. Thereafter, both the child and the therapist independently complete the rating, and then they share their ratings and discuss their rationale. Self-evaluation is taught in order to foster generalization to real-life situations.

Homework. The first several homework problems do not pertain to the child's social problems, and the therapist assigns them merely to establish the homework habit. However, very soon the therapist gives the child homework that entails one of his real-life problems in either his home, his classroom, or on the playground. Each week the therapist reviews the child's homework and either gives tokens for applying the rubric to the situation and arriving at plausible answers or takes away tokens for anything less than good effort.

Modeling. The child is exposed to people who model the use of this self-instruction rubric. Modeling is particularly useful for demonstrating coping strategies when, as sometimes happens in real life,

Figure 8.2
Rating Scale for Use of a Problem-Solving Rubric

How I Did Today

1	2	3	4	5
Not good	OK	Good	Very Good	Super

following the self-instructional rubric does not lead to an effective solution.

Affective Education. Toward the end of the training, the therapist teaches the child to accurately recognize and label his feelings as well as the emotions of others.

Role-Plays. Responses to both hypothetical situations and to real-life situations are frequently role-played. For example, the therapist tells the child, "You are watching a television program and your sister changes the channel. How will you handle this?"

  Key Concept

Successful child-training programs are extensive and therefore labor intensive.

Kendall and Braswell's social-cognitive problem solving is done one-to-one with each child. It is time-consuming and expensive. For example, in a replication of this child-training program, Kazdin and colleagues provided each child with 20 individual sessions, which lasted just short of an hour and occurred over a period of six months.[23] Recognizing the efficiency and expense issues, Kendall and Braswell have discussed ways to do the training using a group format. However, further research is needed to determine the efficacy of social-cognitive problem solving as a group-administered treatment.

Training for Preschool Children

Several researchers developed cognitive-based training programs for preschool children with conduct problems, but the programs failed. However, Carol Webster-Stratton examined these efforts and concluded that the training programs probably were not successful because the material was not developmentally appropriate for preschool children.[24] Therefore, she developed a performance-based intervention designed to appeal to the interests of preschool children. Her training program uses a videotape of more than 100 vignettes showing children in home and school simulations facing and resolving a variety of interpersonal relationship problems, such as controlling their anger, making friends, coping with teasing, and being sent to a time-out area and handling it effectively through self-talk. The training program also involves fantasy play with large puppets, including the ever-popular dinosaurs.

This part of the training program is even called the Dinosaur School. At the Dinosaur School, children are sent to a time-out area for physical aggression and noncompliance, and they also receive rewards for compliance. To develop empathy, after viewing a vignette the children are frequently asked to identify the feelings of the children on the videotape and to discuss possible reasons for their feelings. The weekly sessions also incorporate group activities, role-plays, and stories depicting children solving social problems. The children are taught how to share, to engage in cooperative play, to be friendly, to listen, to comply with requests, to talk about feelings, and to solve interpersonal problems.

During each two-hour session, the children watch approximately 30 minutes of videotape, interspersed with therapist-led discussion of the interactions and skills being modeled. Homework is sent home with the children each week so that, through the use of cue cards, coloring books, cartoons, and stickers, they are reminded to practice the key concepts. At home, parents monitor their child's behavior during the week for performance of specified positive behaviors. The parents reinforce the child when they observe the specified positive behaviors, and they complete behavior charts. At school, the children receive bonus points for bringing their behavior chart from home. Leader manuals and more complete description of the videotapes are available from Dr. Webster-Stratton.[25]

The Dinosaur School training program is labor intensive. Two therapists meet for 22 weekly sessions, each session lasting about two hours with five to six children. The training lasts approximately six months.

Relationship Training for Children with ODD

Children with deeply imbedded oppositional and defiant behaviors are remarkably resistive to any interactions with an adult. They respond with defiance and even aggression whenever any adult attempts even the most benign interaction with them. They do not accept praise. They will not take turns when doing an activity, and they cannot derive enjoyment from participating in a competitive game. No wonder that, according to the research, their parents make few attempts to have positive interactions with them. However, these children need to learn how to participate in a nurturing relationship with an adult.

At our university-based clinic, we work with children ages 3 to 10 years old who have been diagnosed as having severe Oppositional Defiant Disorder (ODD). They have been expelled from day-care programs, preschool, or even kindergarten. If they are of school age, the school is seriously considering an out-of-district placement. Part of the treatment for these children and their parents includes training the child in relationship skills.

The Setting

The clinic room is 13 feet square, and the furnishings are spartan—two small tables, three chairs, and a video camera mounted in the corner next to the ceiling. A 3-foot-by-4-foot one-way mirror hangs on the west wall, and the floor is carpeted. The room has one unusual feature. There is a slide lock near the top of the door—out of the child's reach. The simple furnishings allow the easily distracted child to focus on the clinicians and the few things they bring into the room. With nothing that can be destroyed and full control over the materials, the clinician never has to issue reprimands such as "Don't pull on the picture" or "Please get down from the window ledge." It also helps to slide the lock closed at the top of the door. The child knows there is no escape. In short, everything in the room is designed to elicit the child's cooperation. The room sets the child up for success.

The Clinic Team

Being a university-based clinic, with the training of graduate students as part of the mission, labor is abundant. It is possible to have a supervisor and two well-trained graduate students involved in each hour-long session with the child. The supervisor and a graduate student work directly with the child in the clinic room. One of them takes the role of the lead clinician and deals directly with the child. The other person, the support clinician, handles the materials, uses body positioning to keep the child at his workstation, and occasionally models how a task is performed or the behavior that is expected. The third clinician is the case manager. The case manager accompanies the mother to the observation room and calls the mother's attention to the techniques that the clinician is using to manage the child's behavior. When appropriate, the case manager discusses with the mother how these techniques could be applied in the home. Finally, the case manager is an empathetic listener.

Treatment Approach

We attempt to emulate the caregiving posture described by John McGee as Gentle Teaching.[26] The cardinal principle of Gentle Teaching is that the teacher/therapist must, through his behavior, assure the child that he is emotionally and physically safe in the therapist's presence. The intent of Gentle Teaching is to bond with the child, establish a sense of solidarity, and then progressively guide the child toward participating in a nurturing relationship. Gentle Teaching has nothing to do with content and everything to do with relationship. The materials are simply a medium for establishing a relationship.

The caregiving posture of Gentle Teaching merges nicely with the instructional procedures of Structured Teaching[27] (see Chapter 3), which gives the child visual directives and allows him to anticipate upcoming demands without the therapist having to resort to using verbal directives. Hence, any words that are used during the therapy session, such as labeling or praising, are particularly salient for the child.

Teaching Relationship Skills

To lay the groundwork for teaching relationship skills, the child is first taught a routine. Then he is progressively taught the key relationship skills of (1) being able to have his behavior labeled, (2) willingly accepting praise, (3) participating in cooperative tasks, (4) engaging in turn taking, and (5) being able to enjoy the fellowship of a competitive task.

Learning the Routine. Initially, the child does simple, developmentally appropriate tasks using the Structured Teaching format. During this time, the clinician says very little to the child. It is essential that the child learn the routine and get comfortable with it, because when he has trouble managing the demands of relating, he will collect himself and calm himself by going back to the tasks in the routine, which is comforting.

Labeling. When the child has learned the routine and has discontinued body language that suggests imminent noncompliance or defiance, the clinician uses third-person language to label the child's actions. For example, "Rachel is putting the red ball in the puzzle board." If Rachel does not accept the labeling, she will stop or at least hesitate in the action. Alternatively, if she accepts the labeling, her response will be a little quicker. Finally, it is important to note that the labeling should never resemble praising. For example, the clinician would not say, "Rachel put the ball in the *correct* place."

When Rachel appears to be appreciating the third-person labeling, the clinician switches from third-person to second-person language. "Rachel, *you* put the red ball in the puzzle board." This switching to second-person language frequently elicits passive noncompliance. In that case, the clinician temporarily reverts back to using third-person language to label the actions.

Praise. The clinician then uses the same format and procedures to teach the child to accept and look forward to praise. It is both surprising and instructive to see how incapable these children are of accepting praise. Praising begins by using third-person language (e.g., "Rachel did a nice job putting away the blocks") and then proceeds to using second-person language ("Rachel, you did a nice job putting away the blocks"). Praise needs to be behaviorally specific. The clinician does not say, "Rachel, you did good work." That statement is so vague that it suggests the clinician is not really paying attention. Also, the clinician has to be hesitant about praising only those responses that lead to correct answers (e.g., "Rachel, you put that puzzle piece in the right place. Good going!"). Praising should be about valuing effort (e.g., "You are looking hard for the right piece").

Cooperative Tasks. When the mechanism for valuing the child is established, the clinician introduces cooperative tasks. For example, the clinician might select a more difficult puzzle and actively work with Rachel to complete it. In addition to labeling and giving praise, words are now used to bring fun, enjoyment, and laughter into the relationship. If the usually reserved Rachel jumps up to pop a bubble, the clinician might say, "Wow, Rachel, you jumped so high you almost hit your head on the ceiling."

Turn Taking. When doing cooperative tasks, the clinician gradually relinquishes control until an equitable relationship exists with the child. For example, the clinician initially blows the bubbles and the child pops them. When the child has stopped fighting for control, the clinician progressively relinquishes power until he and the child gradually change roles, and the child is holding the wand and blowing the bubbles and the clinician is popping them. When this relinquishment of power is done properly, the child comes to realize that in an equitable relationship, control does not come from power and dominance; it is obtained through cooperation. Presumably the child also learns that control is not important. What is important is fellowship gained through sharing.

Competitive Games. Finally, the clinician introduces competitive games. Games that have a large element of chance so fortunes can quickly be reversed work best for children with ODD. The competitive game is a vehicle for teaching the child that many interactions have rules that must be followed and that involve turn taking, and someone loses. The child has two lessons to learn. One lesson is how to accept losing. This is best done by modeling. For example, in the game called Trouble, if a player rolls the dice and comes up with a number that will put her on the same spot as an opposing player, the opposing player is knocked back to the starting position. If the clinician rolled a four and it was going to put him on the support clinician's spot, he might say, "Jon, how are you going to react when I bump you back to start?"

"I'll be mad for a brief second," Jon might say, "then I'll remember that going back to start puts me in a position where I can bump you."

"Well then, prepare to go back to start!"

"You'd better look out. I'll be coming after you with the next roll," Jon responds.

When the opportunity comes to bump the child, which the adult can usually see coming before the child does, the clinician uses this same foreshadowing procedure. "Rachel, remember how Jon handled it when he got bumped? How are you going to handle it when you get bumped?"

"I'm gonna tell you to look out for me, 'cause I will then be trying to bump you," she says.

"Well, then," the clinician says, moving his marker, "I am going to give you that chance because I am bumping you."

In the process, the child learns the second lesson: that when competing, the issue is not about who wins and who loses; rather, we sometimes sit down together over a game in order to enjoy each other's company and to build some memories and fun times that can later be shared.

Competing with Peers. Because the child will be expected to play competitive games with other children, it is the final relationship skill taught in the clinic. This is done by first combining several treatment dyads, meaning the children and their mothers. Then the children play a competitive game among themselves with only one adult present.

Involving Parents in the Relationship

At each step of the relationship training, when the child has mastered the skill with the lead clinician, the support clinician leaves the room and the child's mother enters. Most of the time, the mother's involvement immediately causes the child's behavior to markedly regress. Sometimes the child even physically attacks the mother and tries to drive her from the room. However, the clinician calls the child's attention to the routine, and the routine serves to direct the child back to an appropriate behavior and helps him regain self-control. Initially, the mother takes the role of the support clinician, but when the child seems ready, the lead clinician and the parent switch chairs and thus roles. The parent practices providing the nurturing, and the child learns to accept it.

This process is followed for each of the relationship skills. Without exception, every child seen in the clinic had to learn how to accept the nurturing as much or more than the mother needed to learn how to provide it.

Homework Assignments

Homework assignments are given so that the skill being taught in the clinic generalizes to the home. The homework assignment is conveyed to the child and to the mother. Both of them are given responsibilities and expectations. Each of them completes a simple chart, which the clinic has prepared, for each assignment, and they bring the completed chart to the next session.

Principles of Effective Child-Training Programs

The social-cognitive problem-solving model used by Kendall and Braswell, the performance-based training pioneered by Webster-Stratton, and the relationship training done at our clinic are complementary techniques. Any one of them might be selected, depending on the age of the children and the severity of their oppositional and defiant behaviors. The success experienced by these techniques suggests that effective child-training programs incorporate these principles:

- Children need practice in changing their performance in order to change their behavior.

- They need assignments and activities with feedback and monitoring.

- Teachers and parents need to be involved, and they too must give the child feedback.

- The children need to self-monitor their target behaviors.

- Successful treatments are extensive treatments.

 Key Concept

The federal government needs to spearhead the development of a comprehensive treatment program for children with conduct problems and their families, and then find ways to disseminate the program nationwide.

An Idealized Treatment Program

Children with conduct problems are resistant to change. Even the best designed and executed programs report that 30 to 50 percent of the children still have high levels of conduct problems after parent training;[28] even when change is accomplished in the home, it does not generalize to the school;[29] and among the children who initially respond to treatment, the rate of remission after one to two years is high.[30] In short, the current approaches, including our own, sometimes seem like academic exercises. Meanwhile, the number of children with conduct problems who go untreated and are destined for a lifelong pattern of antisocial behavior is nothing short of scary.[31] Comparing the treatment availability to the need is analogous to the little Dutch boy who tried to hold back the sea by sticking his finger in the dike.

An idealized treatment program would be comprehensive. It would consist of a thorough diagnostic assessment followed by appropriate pharmacological treatment and appropriate educational programming including language therapy, if needed, and social-skills training at various developmental stages throughout the child's school career. An idealized treatment program would also consist of parent training, including adjunctive therapy for personal issues such as depression, substance abuse, or marital dysfunction. Finally, the treatment program would also include child training.

Given the number of schoolchildren with conduct problems, the National Institute of Mental Health or the U.S. Department of Education (or perhaps the two organizations working in conjunction) need to spearhead the development of such a comprehensive treatment program. Then they need to train key people in communities to implement the program nationwide.

Notes

[a]Children can have Attention Deficit Disorder (ADD) without the hyperactive component. However, that condition is relatively infrequent. So its more common cousin, ADHD, gets all of the attention (no pun intended) in this book.

[b]A Sign Test is a nonparametric statistic that is, in this situation, used to compare the number of off-task incidents registered by the target child against off-task incidents of the comparison child. For example, if in 20 observations (one every 15 seconds) the target child was off task 12 times whereas the comparison child was not during those same times, then a Sign Test would suggest that the "odds are" (probability of occurrence) that the target child has significantly more off-task behaviors than the comparison child.

[c]A small percentage of children in the early grades have undetected vision problems. If vision problems are present, the child probably is going to have attention problems. With practice, a school psychologist or a school nurse can do a comprehensive vision screening to detect the presence of vision problems.[32]

[d]An extensive body of literature describes the effectiveness of residential treatment programs and daylong, outpatient treatment regimens for adolescents with conduct disorder. This literature is not reviewed here.

9

Developing a Positive School Culture

The first eight chapters of this book present a blueprint for serving oppositional children in schools, and one would like to believe that anyone who faithfully applies these techniques will successfully serve these children. If only that were so. In truth, whether these children succeed depends less on a classroom teacher's techniques and more on her caregiving posture.[1] Some educators innately have the values and beliefs necessary to work successfully with conduct-disordered children, but a few do not.

As the instructional leader, the principal must ensure that each teacher is capable of meeting the educational and developmental needs of every student in the classroom. Creating a positive school climate best does this. This climate could also be called a culture, something that all schools have. A school's culture is so palpable that visitors to the school can "feel" it within 15 minutes of entering the building. Sometimes the culture is created by design, but sometimes it just happens. Cultures that develop by happenstance are seldom ones that elicit staffs' best efforts to progressively and reliably guide children toward success. Ideally, a school's culture is the expression of well-thought-out beliefs and values that the educators in the school hold in common about how children should be educated.

The core beliefs and values found in a school that is positioned to work successfully with conduct-disordered children can readily be specified. In general terms, the educators must believe that the art of teaching is about more than teaching reading, writing, and arithmetic. Education also includes enhancing children's ability to develop and maintain nurturing relationships with adults and mutually beneficial relationships with peers. The staff unfailingly believe in preserving the child's dignity, even when they are managing inappropriate behavior. They convey to children that they, the children, are what is important. The educators understand the importance of valuing the whole child. When taking the measure of a child, they innately see the child's attributes and potential, not just the problems. The educators believe that how much a child learns and how well he behaves are, in part, indices of the quality of the teacher-student bond.

More specifically, six values and beliefs characterize educators who can work successfully with conduct-disordered children.[2] Three of these pertain to helping children grow socially, emotionally, and academically; and the other three reflect the approach that the educator instinctively uses to manage children's inappropriate behaviors.

 Key Concept

When it comes to working successfully with children who have behavior problems, the most important and indispensable factor is having staff who have the "right stuff."

Values and Beliefs That Promote Social, Emotional, and Academic Growth

Ensuring Success

No matter how low children's skill level may be, the educator values children for the social, emotional, and academic skills they can demonstrate, and provides the structure, support, and recognition children need to demonstrate those skills.[3]

In their classic work, *400 Losers*, Ahlstrom and Havighurst followed 400 youths from 7th grade through high school and documented all of the factors that contributed to their destiny.[4] Half of the boys were enrolled in an extensive work-study program, and the other half, which represented the control group, were not. Surprisingly, the intensive work-study program was not effective. However, a few adolescents in the work-study group escaped what seemed to be their predetermined fate. What was the difference for this small group? The difference was a mentor. The youths who "made it" were lucky enough to have had a few select teachers who valued them. These teachers were patient but determined, meaning they never gave up on the boys. They were flexible in teaching, personable, and able to adapt to the needs of the boys. In other words, they did more than teach the academic skills.

Ensuring success means the educator endeavors to make the children socially, emotionally, and academically successful. Educators who believe in ensuring success recognize that these children often come to school unmotivated to gain knowledge and acquire information—the things that schools traditionally do. Instead, these children sometimes come to school with unmet, more basic needs. Instead of being motivated to learn to read that day, they need to feel safe and secure. Instead of wanting to learn their addition facts, they need to feel wanted and accepted. Unfortunately, these children can seldom articulate these needs. Instead, they yell, throw things, glare, or sulk. The educator who believes in ensuring success correctly interprets these problematic behaviors as the children's primitive attempts to communicate their needs, and responds accordingly. These educators are willing to postpone academic learning while they give children the support they need in order to be ready to acquire information and gain knowledge.

Independent Decision Making

Effective educators believe in allowing children to make decisions independently and then to experience the natural consequence of those decisions, be they good or bad.[5]

Making decisions is a great learning tool. If the child makes a good decision, the teacher has an opportunity to acknowledge the decision and thereby increase the likelihood that the child will make similar decisions in the future. Acknowledging a good decision also values the child and thereby further increases the bond. However, learning also occurs when the child makes a wrong decision. Learning that stems from making a "wrong" decision is epitomized in an often-repeated story about Thomas Edison. Reputedly, someone once asked Mr. Edison how he invented the electric lightbulb. Edison responded with a detailed explanation of his extensive efforts and all of his unsuccessful attempts before he finally hit on the right combination of things that, when electricity was passed through the filament, produced continuous light. "I see," the inquisitor said. "You had many failures before you finally had success." Edison sharply responded, "No. I did not have a single failure! I had many experiments that taught me what I needed to know."

Children can be "wrong" in endless ways. A child who goes out for recess on a cold day without a coat is "wrong." The child who attempts to pour every bit of a half-pint of milk into a small cup is "wrong." The educator who understands the principle of independent decision making does not correct these poor decisions. Rather, the educator allows the child the dignity of making a poor decision and then, when the child is ready, provides the information, skills, and support needed to make a better decision next time.

🔑 Key Concept

Children learn more from making mistakes than they learn when an educator tells them what to do.

Allowing children to make decisions not only gives them the opportunity to learn, it does so in a way that preserves their dignity. It is critical to have staff who instinctively allow children to make independent decisions because oppositional children don't like to be told what to do. However, the principle of independent decision making comes with a caveat. Children cannot be allowed to make decisions that would endanger someone's health, safety, or welfare; portend damage to property; or impose on someone's basic rights.

Teaching for Behavior Change

Teaching for behavior change is the proactive process of helping a child replace problematic behaviors with appropriate behaviors. It is accomplished by having empathy for the child, identifying the underlying deficit, breaking that deficit into teachable components, and setting up positive learning experiences.[6]

Educators who can work effectively with oppositional children instinctively do not pay excessive attention to a persistent problematic behavior, but instead focus on the child's underlying deficit. The deficit is always a missing skill, a lack of information, or a misguided value system.

 Key Concept

Most persistent problematic behavior occurs because the child has a skill deficit, and the best approach to changing the behavior is to mitigate that deficit.

An Academic Skill Deficit

Cassandra occasionally got up from her desk and walked out of the classroom. At first, it seemed like she was intentionally defying the teacher's authority and not following the rules. With that mind-set, the teacher thought about punishing Cassandra when she walked out of the classroom by having her stay in during recess. However, the teacher was not comfortable with that solution. She asked for someone to observe in the classroom to see if there was an antecedent for Cassandra's leaving the classroom.

There was. Cassandra often left the room whenever the teacher gave any assignment that involved reading. Informal assessment determined that Cassandra had only 10 words in her reading vocabulary, which led the teacher to hypothesize that Cassandra left the room because she had a skill deficit in reading.

The deficit is not always an academic skill. Harry had a persistent problematic behavior because he did not have the needed skills to get along with his peers.

A Social Skill Deficit

During the noon hour, when the 6th graders generally played softball, Harry often got into an altercation with another student. The altercation was invariably precipitated by Harry's malicious remarks (e.g., "Hey, my grandmother can catch better than that").

From the perspective of teaching for behavior change, it was easy to have empathy for Harry. He had no friends, and it is tough to be a 12-year-old and not have friends. Specifically, instead of deriding his teammates, Harry needed to learn how to give small but appropriate compliments that encouraged them. It also wouldn't hurt if he became a better softball player.

A few private sessions were set up with the softball coach to improve Harry's catching and hitting skills, and, more to the point, the school counselor and Harry watched and discussed videos designed to instill in him a sense of how it feels to be the recipient of mean-spirited comments. The counselor taught Harry some complimentary comments he could say to his teammates, such as "good catch" and "nice throw." She and Harry role-played using these positive comments in one-to-one training, and Harry rehearsed and then implemented them. On the playground, things improved for Harry.

Persistent patterns of problematic behavior can also be caused by a lack of information or at least not taking the time to think through the implications of an action. Sam's problematic behavior occurred because he never considered the effects of his actions.

A Lack of Information

Sam, a 6th grader, came thundering down the school's wooden stairs. When he reached the bottom, the principal was there to greet him. "Sam," she scolded, "for that antic, you can stay in during recess and walk up and down those stairs 25 times! Every time you get to the bottom, you write this sentence: 'I will never again run down the stairs.'"

The principal's solution had mixed success. Sam did stay in for the start of recess, and he did walk up and down the stairs several times, each time writing the sentence, "I will never again run down the stairs." However, after the fifth trip down the stairs, he simply wrote the remaining 20 sentences, signed his name, and went out for recess. When the principal came to monitor her miscreant student, she found the 25 sentences with Sam's signature at the bottom, but she noted that he had completed the punishment in five minutes. Knowing that he had cheated, she went looking for him.

If the principal had asked herself, "What do I know about running down the stairs that Sam does not know?" she would have attributed Sam's problematic behavior to a lack of information. Namely, Sam probably never thought about how running down stairs could endanger himself or other smaller children, and he definitely did not think about how the noise disrupted other students. If the principal had had this mind-set, she would have said, "Sam, the school has a rule against running in the building. I'd like you to spend some time thinking about why the school has this rule and jot down your thoughts. Tomorrow, you can stop by my office and share your thoughts with me."

The next day, Sam would have been able to relate several good reasons why the school has a rule against running in the building, and the principal could have honestly told Sam that she was impressed by his insights. She might even have asked Sam to share his thoughts with the 1st graders and to design and implement a short skills-training program so that the little kids could understand why they should not run in the building. The teaching-for-behavior-change approach would have equipped Sam with the understandings he needed to inhibit his temptation to thunder down the stairs, it would have preserved his dignity, and, in the end, it would have conveyed a sense that the principal valued him.

 Key Concept

Valuing a child for a particular behavior seems to biologically inhibit the child from doing anything to betray that trust.

Occasionally a persistent problematic behavior is caused by the child's value system. When this is the case, the child usually has a parent-supported value system that differs markedly from the mainstream value system. Examples include smoking, drug use, alcohol use, improper treatment of women, and, sometimes, aggression.

A Conflicting Value System

If a student brushed against Jerry's desk, he kicked the student. If a student slipped into the lunch line ahead of him, Jerry pulled the kid out of line and punched him. In short, any time another child did something that Jerry interpreted as imposing on his rights, he attacked him or her. To make matters worse, Jerry continued to be aggressive toward his peers despite his teacher's best efforts.

At her wits' end, the principal called Jerry's parents into school to discuss Jerry's aggressive behaviors and to inform them that the school was on the verge of removing Jerry from his regular classroom and placing him in a room for emotionally disturbed children. As the principal reviewed each specific incident of Jerry's aggressive behavior, Mr. Jensen became increasingly agitated. Finally, he had all he could take. Slamming his fist down on the table, Mr. Jensen exclaimed, "That's right, ma'am. I'm not raisin' no god-damned sissy."

Jerry's aggression toward other children was fed by his stepfather's value system, which included sticking up for oneself in a belligerent manner. In Mr. Jensen's opinion, anyone who didn't stick up for his rights was a fool and a sissy. So when the teacher tried to help Bran-don curb his aggression, Jerry simply concluded that his teacher was another one of those "sissies."[a]

When a child with severe behavior problems engages in inappro-priate behavior, educators who can work effectively with such chil-dren react in a characteristic way. They

- Have empathy for the child;
- Develop a hypothesis about the child's deficit;
- Break the deficit into components; and
- Set up and implement positive, errorless learning experiences to address each component.

Values and Beliefs That Guide Educators in Managing Inappropriate Behavior

No Punishment

We maintain that *punishment is anything that is done to intentionally make children feel guilty, humiliated, remorseful, or fearful in an attempt to get them to change their behavior.*[7]

 Key Concept

To be effective with oppositional children, educators must manage the children's problematic behaviors without resorting to punishment.

Of the six beliefs and values, the most important is the belief that children should not be punished. However, not using punishment to change behavior begs the question, "What is an educator to do?" As mentioned in Chapter 7, there are effective ways to respond to problematic behavior that do not involve punishment. They involve using the last two beliefs and values: gentle interventions and logical consequences.

Gentle Interventions

When a child engages in behavior that threatens health, safety, property, or basic rights, then staff must, at that moment, do only what is necessary to disrupt the behavior.

A school must have educators who can skillfully defuse problematic behavior instead of doing things that provoke it. Educators who do not believe in punishing children and who endeavor to ensure the child's success tend to use gentle interventions. That is, they ignore the problematic behavior and redirect the child toward some appropriate action that can be acknowledged and praised.

Logical Consequences

A logical consequence is the relationship between how a child behaves and what, by intent or necessity, happens as a result. A logical consequence can be positive, such as when responsible behavior warrants an additional privilege, or a logical consequence can mean a loss of privileges to the extent necessary to protect health, safety, property, and basic rights.[8]

A logical consequence is not a punishment. It is a loss of privileges, and it is a loss of privileges *only* to the extent necessary to protect people, property, and basic rights. For example, when the 2nd-grade class is dismissed for lunch, Billy often races down the hall. His stomping feet disturb other classes, and he is going so fast that if a classroom door suddenly swung open, he'd run into it. Something must be done. Billy needs to lose certain privileges, but only to the extent that the loss will stop him from disrupting other classes and prevent him from running headlong into a door or over a child. Staying in during recess would not be a logical consequence; it would be a punishment designed to make him think twice about running in the hallway. Instead, his teacher should explain to Billy how his running disturbs others and endangers smaller children, and then she should tell him that until she helps him gain the self-control that it takes to walk in the hallway, he will need to stay at the back of the line and walk beside her as they go to lunch.

Developing a Vision and Mission Statement

Schools often incorporate their core values and beliefs in a mission. Establishing a vision and a mission helps to define the school's culture.

A vision is futuristic, possibly so idealistic as to be not wholly obtainable, but definitely worth striving for. In the case of educating oppositional children, a plausible vision would be equipping these children with the relationship skills necessary for them to be motivated to gain knowledge and increase their understanding of the world.

After a vision has been established, the next step is to articulate the mission. A mission is an easily remembered statement that answers the question, "Why does our school exist?" A mission statement is also a screen that every worker in the school uses daily to guide decisions and actions. For example, a plausible mission for a school that wants to work effectively with behaviorally challenged children would be this: "We prepare *all* students to succeed."

A mission statement that sits on a shelf or is posted in the hallway and forgotten is of no value. A school does not have a meaningful mission if most of the people working in the building cannot state it. To be in the employees' minds, the mission has to be acted upon. Thus, hiring people who accept and can willingly enact the mission is critical.

Hiring Staff with the Requisite Beliefs and Values

Administrators have long known that they can develop a person's skills, but it is very difficult to change an employee's attitude. Or, to put it in the clearest terms, people who can work effectively with behaviorally challenged children are not trained, they are hired.[9] The principal must hire and retain staff whose inherent value system is supportive of developing and fostering nurturing relationships with children. Furthermore, *everyone* who works in the building—not just the certified staff—must support the development of nurturing relationships with children; for everyone, including the classroom aides, the cook, the janitor, the secretary, and the bus drivers, interacts daily with children and contributes to the school's climate.

Situational questions are an excellent tool for determining whether an applicant has the six requisite beliefs and values. For example, we have developed a set of 24 such situational questions. The 24 questions are arranged in four sets of six situational questions that pertain to one of the six core values (i.e., ensuring success, independent decision making, teaching for behavior change, no punishment, gentle interventions, and logical consequences). The four sets are arranged in order of increasing difficulty. The questions in the first two sets determine whether the applicant inherently has a value system that is consistent with developing nurturing relationships with children. The questions in the last two sets gauge whether the applicant has the skills to implement each particular core value. For example, the first question in the first set examines the applicant's attitude about no punishment. The question is: "As a state legislator, would you vote for or against a law permitting an educator to, under certain circumstances, spank a child? Why?" In the fourth and final set, the applicant is asked another question about punishment. This question is designed to determine whether the applicant can manage problematic behavior without resorting to punishment. The question is: "A visitor to the school tells you that she saw Craig, a behavior-disturbed 3rd-grade boy, take some change from the top of his teacher's desk. As Craig's teacher, how would you handle this?" This is a difficult question, and few applicants give a good answer; but if someone does, hire that applicant!

In general, applicants who give good answers to the situational questions in Set 1 and Set 2 have the requisite inherent value system and should be hired. Their value system about interpersonal relationships is compatible with a school that endeavors to take a humanistic approach toward children. Applicants who do well on Set 3 and Set 4 have both the requisite value system about educating children with behavior problems and the skills to develop nurturing relationships with the children.

Hiring has implications for establishing the vision. In order for the stakeholders to develop and endorse a vision and articulate a mission that will attend to the needs of conduct-disordered children, a vocal majority of the staff must inherently have a value and belief system about children that is compatible with the six core values and beliefs.

Training

Not many applicants answer every situational question perfectly. However, administrators can hire people who have the right value system but lack the skills to implement those values if they provide supplemental training. Among other advantages, the buildingwide training establishes a common vocabulary among the staff. For example, it becomes common for staff in the teachers lounge to talk about such topics as independent decision making and logical consequences.

Aligning Supervision, Policies, and Procedures

The final step in creating a school culture that meets the needs of behaviorally disturbed children is to explicitly state the job expectations and then provide supervision so that the staff get direct feedback about their job performance.[10] Of course, the school must have supporting policies and procedures. When the school has a mission that supports a humanistic approach to educating the whole child, hires staff whose inherent value system about interpersonal relationships is compatible with that mission, trains and supervises the staff to enhance their skills, and has aligned policies and procedures and rewards to support that mission, then a truly beautiful thing happens. Everyone in the school starts helping students succeed. Then the mission is being implemented, the school has the requisite culture, and the techniques we suggest in the first eight chapters will start to work.

Note

[a]When the parents' value system differs so sharply from the social norms, it places the school in a difficult position. The anecdote "A Conflicting Value System" is a case in point. Like all vignettes in the book, it is true. The solution was to tell the stepdad that aggression was not acceptable at school, and if Jerry continued to physically attack other children, it would be necessary to remove him from the classroom and place him in a self-contained classroom for emotionally disturbed children. Furthermore, the school district's self-contained classroom was across town. It would be necessary for a bus to pick Jerry up in the morning and bring him home at the end of the school day. The principal went on to say that because Mr. Jensen believed in fighting, Jerry was certain to continue to be aggressive. She saw no need to wait for another incident and would immediately start making arrangements for the placement. This got Mr. Jensen's attention. He did not want Jerry removed from his class and placed in another school. Striking a contemplative posture, the principal announced that there was one alternative to try before making the placement. Mr. Jensen impatiently asked what it was. The principal replied that she would suspend placement if the Jensens took Jerry to family counseling at the mental health center. The goal for the counseling, she explained, would be that they and Jerry would explore alternative ways for Jerry to respond when he perceived someone was taking advantage of him. The principal concluded by saying that if they went to counseling and if, two months later, Jerry's physical aggression did not pose a danger to other students, he could stay in his regular classroom.

This story had a good ending. The parents went to counseling, Mr. Jensen enrolled in an alcohol treatment program, and Jerry's aggression at school subsided.

Epilogue

Childhood is a time for protecting, indulging, and nurturing children, but it is not without purpose. During this stage of development children are expected to acquire the learning and the behaviors that are consistent with society's larger belief system. In the United States, this responsibility for instructing children is shared equally between the home, which is expected to instill values, morals, a work ethic, and relationship skills, and the school, which is expected to teach children how to read, write, and do arithmetic. For the first three hundred years of U.S. public education, this delegation of responsibilities worked well. With few exceptions, parents sent children to school who were generally obedient, respectful, and mindful of their looming responsibilities. The children came to school primed and ready to learn academic subject matter. At school, educators did a masterful job of teaching them. By the time children graduated from high school, they were prepared to accept and manage adult responsibilities.

However, with recent societal changes an increasingly larger percentage of children (an estimated 5 to 10 percent of the student body) come to school ill prepared to learn academic subject matter. When educators attempt to teach, these children throw temper tantrums and refuse to work. They become defiant, noncompliant, belligerent, and aggressive. They not only do not learn academics, but they become so disruptive that they markedly interfere with the education of other students. Even though their numbers are few, their behavior is so severe that, as a group, these children have created a crisis in education.

This book describes techniques that educators will find useful in responding to oppositional children. The techniques will mitigate the frequency and intensity of noncompliant behaviors by giving these children support and structure. The techniques will also help the teacher with the daily management of the classroom. However, these techniques do not get at the root causes of why the children resist being in school. These children are resistive about doing schoolwork because they are not ready to learn academic skills. They have been dropped off on the school's doorstep without the requisite values, work ethic, sense of responsibility, or relationship skills. So when educators "teach" them, these children scream, holler, have temper tantrums, and throw things in a primitive attempt to communicate that their needs are not being met. Before they memorize addition facts, these children want to know that they are emotionally safe in the educator's presence. Before they think about the meaning of a reading passage, they need assurances that they are valued and accepted. Before they learn to write a story, they need to know that someone cares about their story. These children do not need "teachers." They need educators who will patiently show them, primarily through modeling, how to develop and maintain a nurturing relationship and who will then use that relationship as the foundation upon which to instill values, morals, and a work ethic.

Just as educators benefited when, with the passage of Public Law 94-142 in 1975, they were asked to teach *all* children, they similarly will be rewarded by learning how to work effectively with oppositional children. Educators who learn to work effectively with these children will, in the process, develop a high level of emotional maturity. They will gain understandings about human relationships that will benefit them far beyond the classroom.

However, on the other side of the ledger (the debit side) educators must accept that they can have only a limited impact on the lives of the conduct-disordered children who pass through their classrooms. School did not cause these children to be oppositional and defiant. School is simply a situation that places sufficient demands on these children that they have to face their personal shortcomings. These children need a comprehensive treatment program that, in addition to tailored educational programming, includes, at minimum, parent training, child training, and possibly psychopharmacological supports.

Without all of these services, an oppositional child is very likely to grow up to be an antisocial adult.

However, the common thread that binds educators is that they care about children. They will not rest easy knowing that no agency or institution in the community is providing the comprehensive treat-ment services that these oppositional children need. It may take time, but schools will eventually take the lead in providing comprehensive treatment services for oppositional and defiant children.

Glossary

Antecedents—Events that occur just before a particular behavior, the target behavior, is displayed. For example, a teacher's saying no to an oppositional child often is an antecedent for the child's aggression.

Antisocial Personality Disorder—A personality disorder characterized by a disregard for and violation of other people's rights.

Asperger's Syndrome—A disorder characterized by problems interpreting subtle social cues and therefore difficulty with interpersonal relationships. People with Asperger's Syndrome characteristically have a narrow range of interests; however, they often have an intense, almost driving interest in a few selected, often arcane, topics. They usually have gross motor problems that, in children, manifest themselves as a reluctance to do written work.

At Risk—A term used to describe students who are achieving below grade level and are likely to experience educational, social, emotional, or mental health problems in the future.

Attention Deficit Hyperactivity Disorder (ADHD)—A disorder characterized by problems completing assignments, attending to tasks, and retaining focus, and associated with excessive and interfering motor movements.

Autism—A pervasive developmental disorder characterized by extreme unresponsiveness to others, poor communication skills, limited skill at imaginative play, and odd or bizarre reactions to the environment.

Aversive Stimulus—A stimulus that hurts or doesn't feel good. It is assumed that the recipient of an aversive stimulus will change his or her behavior in response to it. For example, spanking a child for walking into the street is assumed to be applying an aversive stimulus. All aversive stimuli are assumed to entail punishment, but not all punishment entails aversive stimuli.

Behavior—The response that an organism makes to the stimuli in its environment.

Behavior Modification (Behaviorism)—A theory predicated on the belief that behavior can be explained and predicted in terms of responses to external stimuli. The basic principle is that behaviors can be modified by reinforcement contingencies.

Clinical Depression—A low, sad state in which life, despite evidence to the contrary, seems bleak and its challenges appear to be overwhelming.

Cognitive-Behavior Model—A theoretical perspective that emphasizes the process and content of the thinking that underlies behavior.

Conduct Disorder—A pathological pattern of childhood behavior in which the child repeatedly violates the basic rights of others or of major societal norms or rules by displaying aggressive behavior, destroying property, lying, or running away from home.

Control Group—A group of subjects in an experiment who are not exposed to the presumably critical treatment.

Correlation—The degree to which events vary in comparison with each other.

Diagnosis—The process of determining the cause for a person's pathology.

Extinction—Stopping the reinforcement contingency for a response, which will, according to behaviorist theory, result in a decrease in the response rate.

Foreshadowing—An indication of a coming event. For example, when a teacher says, "Art will be over in two minutes," the students know that they should start planning the end of their art project. Many students with conduct problems do not respond well to sudden changes in their schedule. They need foreshadowing.

Fragile X Syndrome—A chromosomal disorder characterized by moderate to severe mental retardation, language impairments, and behavior problems.

Generalization—A particular way of responding to a stimulus. There are two types of generalizations. *Response generalization* is the act of making a similar but related response to the same stimulus. For example, a child might meet a teacher in the hallway and say, "Hi." Later, the child might meet the same teacher in the hallway and say, "Good morning." The other type of generalization is *stimulus generalization*, which is the act of giving the same response to somewhat different stimuli. The student might meet Ms. Jones in the hallway and say, "Hi." Later, he might meet Mrs. Schmidt in the hallway and say, "Hi."

Generalized Anxiety Disorder—A disorder characterized by general and persistent feelings of anxiety and worry about numerous events and activities.

Gentle Teaching—A caregiving posture whose principal developer is Dr. John McGee. The tenet of Gentle Teaching is that, regardless of the child's behavior, the clinician or teacher must respond in ways that assure the child that he or she is physically and emotionally safe in the caregiver's presence. The goal of Gentle Teaching is to "bond" with the child.

Humanist Model—The theoretical perspective that humans are born with a natural inclination to be friendly, cooperative, and constructive, and are driven to self-actualize.

IEP—See Individualized Educational Program/Plan.

Ignoring—The absence of a response that is believed to reinforce a particular undesirable behavior. Behaviorists believe that if a response persists, it is being reinforced. For example, a student makes obnoxious noises when the teacher is writing on the blackboard because the behavior causes the teacher to stop writing, wheel around, and say, "Okay. Who did that?" The student gets a reaction from the teacher and thereby knows that he is in control of her behavior. The principle of ignoring would call for the teacher to stop responding on the premise that if the behavior is not reinforced, it will stop (extinguish).

Individualized Educational Program/Plan (IEP)—A program or plan designed by a team of educators and the child's parents to meet the unique needs of a child with special needs. Every student who qualifies for extra or "special" services must have an IEP. The IEP states broad goals, such as better peer relations, and then lists specific objectives that, if fulfilled, result in achieving the broad goal.

Intelligence Quotient (IQ)—A number system used to indicate the level of a person's mental ability wherein 100 is average.

Intermittent Explosive Disorder—An impulse-control disorder in which people periodically fail to resist aggressive impulses, leading to the performance of serious assaults on people or destruction of property.

Law of Effect—The principle that states that when a response leads to a satisfying consequence, it is strengthened and is likely to be repeated.

Learning Disability—A disorder of delayed development in one or more of the processes of thinking, speaking, reading, writing, listening, or doing arithmetic operations.

Main Streaming—The provision of accommodations that enable children with special needs to be educated in the same classroom as their same-age cohorts.

Master Teacher—A teacher who is given special status, pay, and recognition but remains in the classroom as a role model for other teachers or is sometimes released from a portion of regular classroom assignments to work with other teachers.

Mood Disorder—One of several specific disorders, including depression and Bipolar Disorder, that affect one's emotional state.

Obsessive-Compulsive Disorder—A disorder in which a person has recurrent and unwanted thoughts or the need to perform repetitive and ritualistic actions, and the experience of intense anxiety whenever these behaviors are suppressed.

Operant Conditioning—Procedures wherein a response is systematically followed by a reward, extinction, or punishment. Operant conditioning theorists believe that it is the consequence that follows a response that determines its frequency, and that behavior consists of responses. If one can control the response rate, one can change behavior.

Oppositional Defiant Disorder—A disorder in which children argue repeatedly with adults, lose their temper, and feel great anger and resentment.

Overcorrection—A contingency on inappropriate behavior that requires the person to engage in an effortful response that more than corrects the effects of the inappropriate behavior. For example, a child who urinates on the bathroom floor is given a rag and pail of hot water and required to clean the entire bathroom floor.

Pediatric Psychiatrist—A physician who, in addition to medical school, has completed three to four years of residency training in the treatment of children with abnormal mental and behavior functioning.

Placebo—A sham treatment that the patient believes is genuine. Sugar is a commonly used substance in a placebo pill.

P.L. 94-142—The Education of All Handicapped Children Act, which Congress passed in 1975 and which requires all schools receiving federal dollars to provide an appropriate education in the least (possible) restrictive setting for students with handicapping conditions.

Pragmatics—A term used by speech and language pathologists to describe using all of the available information, such as facial expressions, social context, relationship with the speaker, etc., to determine the meaning of a communication.

Premack Principle—A principle that states that the opportunity to engage in a high-frequency behavior could reinforce the occurrence of a low-frequency behavior. The Premack Principle has also been called "Grandma's Law"—i.e., you have to eat your peas (a low-frequency behavior) before you can have ice cream (a high-frequency behavior). David Premack developed the principle in his work with rats.

Prevalence—The total number of cases of a problem or a disorder occurring in a population over a specific period of time.

Prompt—A supplemental stimulus that raises the probability of a correct response.

Punishment—Behaviorists define punishment as a response contingency that serves to decrease the probability of a response. Taking a humanistic perspective, we believe that punishment is anything a caregiver does to a child that is intended to make the child feel so bad, guilty, or remorseful that he or she is not likely to make that response again.

Reality Therapy—A therapy developed by William Glasser and based on the premise that a person is responsible for his or her situation. Reality Therapy follows a chain of logic to show a person how he or she engaged in behavior that brought about the current, usually unsatisfactory, situation and then suggests how the person can take responsibility for his or her behavior, change it, and achieve a more satisfying outcome.

Response Cost—A type of punishment designed to decrease the frequency of a response by taking away reinforcers that the child has accumulated. Response cost is often used in conjunction with a token economy system. The child might earn 10 chips for completing an assignment, but could lose 5 for getting up from his desk without permission.

Response Set—A mind-set for making a particular response. For example, when driving, most people have a response set to take their foot off the accelerator and put it on the brake when they come to a red light. They do not have this particular response set when walking through a shopping mall.

Role-Play—A therapy technique that entails patients' or clients' acting out how they intend to respond to situations that they are likely to experience.

Setting Events—According to George Sugai, one of the first applied behaviorists to use this term, setting events are the environmental cues, taken in total context, that set the stage for particular behaviors. For example, a funeral is a setting event for grief. The beginning of class should be a setting event for listening to teachers in order to gain information.

Socialized Conduct Disorder—A Conduct Disorder is a pattern of aggressive, antisocial behavior that affects the public. Examples of conduct-disordered behaviors are stealing and vandalism. When these actions are done as part of a group or a gang, the adolescent is said to have a *Socialized Conduct Disorder.*

Socially Promoted—An expression commonly used by educators to indicate that a child did not achieve the academic skills taught at a particular grade level but was promoted to the next grade level in order to stay with his or her same-age peers.

Social Skills Training—A therapeutic approach used by school counselors and school psychologists to help children acquire or improve their social skills through the use of role-playing and rehearsing desirable behaviors.

Structured Teaching—A system used by Division TEACCH (Treatment and Education of Autistic and Related Communication-handicapped Children) at the University of North Carolina to instruct children with autism. Structured Teaching is a method of presenting learning tasks to students with autism in such a way that, by looking, they know what needs to be done, how much needs to be done, and when it is finished. Structured Teaching has nothing to do with *what* to teach, but everything to do with *how* to teach.

Task Analysis—Breaking a complex behavior into smaller component parts such that the parts, when combined, equal the whole.

Time-out—Removal from access to reinforcement. In school, time-out usually means a child must go somewhere, such as a time-out area in the back of the room, for a set period and until he or she is sufficiently calm to rejoin the class.

Token—Some object that represents a more fundamental reward that will be given in the future. In schools, poker chips are often given for good behavior. At the end of the day, the poker chips can be exchanged for something that the children value, such as candy, toys, or time to play computer games.

Token Economy—A system of learned secondary reinforcers that the child receives and can later exchange for a variety of reinforcers.

Tropism—Movements that animals (or plants) make with reference to the direction of a stimulus. *Taxis*, a synonym, is more commonly used to describe the movement of animals with reference to the direction of a stimulus; *tropism* is more commonly used to describe the movement of plants. However, the terms are often used interchangeably.

Undersocialized Conduct Disorder—A diagnosis given to adolescents who have a pattern of aggressive, antisocial behavior that affects the public, but they engage in such behaviors alone and not as part of a group or gang.

Verbal Prompt—A supplemental verbal stimulus that raises the probability of a correct response.

References

Chapter 1

1. American Psychiatric Association (1980). *Diagnostic and statistical manual of mental disorders, DSM-III* (3rd ed.). Washington, DC: Author.

2. Eron, L. D., Gentry, J. H., & Schlegel, P. (Eds.). (1994). *Reason to hope: A psychosocial perspective on violence & youth.* Washington, DC: American Psychological Association.

3. U.S. Department of Education (1989). *Youth Indicators, 1988.* Washington, DC: U.S. Government Printing Office.

4. Crowther, J. K., Bond, L. A., & Rolf, J. E. (1981). The incidence, prevalence, and severity of behavior disorders among preschool-aged children in day care. *Journal of Abnormal Child Psychology, 9,* 23–42.

5. Staub, E. (1996). Cultural-societal roots of violence: The examples of genocidal violence and of contemporary youth violence in the United States. *American Psychologist, 51*(2), 117–131.

6. Administration for Children and Families (2002). Temporary assistance for needy families (TANF): Percent of total U.S. population, 1960–1999. Accessed November 27, 2002, at http://www.acf.dhhs.gov/news/stats/6097rf.htm.

7. National Center for Children in Poverty (1999). Accessed November 2001 at http://cpmcnet.columbia.edu/dept/nccp/99uptext.html.

8. Dishion, T. J., Patterson, G. R., Stoolmiller, M., & Skinner, M. L. (1991). Family, school, and behavior antecedents to early adolescent involvement with antisocial peers. *Developmental Psychology, 27*(1), 172–180.

9. Webster-Stratton, C. (1989). The relationship of marital support, conflict, and divorce to parent perceptions, behavior, and childhood conduct problems. *Journal of Marriage and the Family, 51,* 417–430.

10. Eron, L. D. (1963). Relationship of TV viewing habits and aggressive behavior in children. *Journal of Abnormal and Social Psychology, 67*(2), 1993–1996.

11. Hughes, J. N. (1996). Television violence: Implications for violence prevention. *School Psychology Review, 25*(2), 134–151.

12. Joy, L. A., Kimball, M. M., & Zabrack, M. L. (1986). Television and children's aggressive behavior. In T. M. Williams (Ed.), *The impact of television: A natural experiment in three communities* (pp. 303–360). Orlando, FL: Academic Press Inc.

13. Huesmann, L. R. (1986). Psychological processes promoting the relation between

exposure to media violence and aggressive behavior by the viewer. *Journal of Social Issues, 42*(3), 125–139.

14. Viemeroe, V. (1996). Factors in childhood that predict later criminal behavior. *Aggressive Behavior, 22*(2), 87–97.

15. Matlock, J. R., & Green, V. P. (1990). The effects of day care on the social and emotional development of infants, toddlers and preschoolers. *Early Child Development and Care, 64,* 55–59.

16. Belksy, J. (1990). Developmental risks associated with infant day care: Attachment insecurity, noncompliance, and aggression? In S. Chehrazi (Ed.), *Psychosocial issues in day care* (pp. 37–68). Washington, DC: American Psychiatric Press, Inc.

17. Dettling, A. C., Gunnar, M. R., & Donsella, B. (1999). Cortisol levels of young children in full-day childcare centers: Relations with age and temperament. *Psychoneuroendocrinology, 24*(5), 519–536.

18. Goldstein, N. E., Arnold, D. H., Rosenberg, J. L., Stowe, R. M., & Ortiz, C. (2001). Contagion of aggression in day care classrooms as a function of peer and teacher responses. *Journal of Educational Psychology, 93*(4), 708–719.

19. Luria, A. R. (1981). *Language and cognition* (J. V. Wertsch, Trans.). New York: John Wiley & Sons. (Original work published 1979.)

20. Jakobson, R. (1968). *Child language, aphasia and phonological universals* (A. Keiler, Trans.). The Hague: Mouton. (Original work published 1941.)

21. Chomsky, N. (1957). *Syntactic structures.* The Hague: Mouton.

22. Huesmann L. R., Eron, L. D., Lefkowitz, M. M., & Walder, J. O. (1984). The stability of aggression over time and generations. *Developmental Psychology, 20*(6), 1120–1134.

23. Olweus, D. (1979). Stability of aggressive reaction patterns in males: A review. *Psychological Bulletin, 86,* 852–857.

24. Lee, C., & Bates, J. (1985). Mother-child interactions at age two years and perceived difficult temperament. *Child Development, 56,* 1314–1326.

25. Richman, N., Stevenson, J., & Graham, P. J. (1983). *Preschool to school: A behavioral study.* London: Academic Press.

26. Maziade, M., Cote, R., Bernier, H., Boutin, P., & Thiverge, J. (1989). Significance of extreme temperament in infancy for clinical status in preschool years: I. Value of extreme temperament at 4–8 months for predicting diagnosis at 4.7 years. *Journal of Psychiatry, 154,* 535–543.

27. White, J. L., Moffit, T. E., Earls, F., Robins, L., & Silva, P. (1990). How early can we tell? Predictors of childhood conduct disorder and adolescent delinquency. *Criminology, 28*(4), 507–528.

28. Werry, J. S., & Quay, H. C. (1971). The prevalence of behavior symptoms in younger elementary school children. *American Journal of Orthopsychiatry, 4,* 136–143.

29. Mitchell, S., & Rosa, P. (1981). Boyhood behavior problems as precursors of criminality: A fifteen-year follow-up study. *Journal of Child Psychology and Psychiatry, 22,* 19–33.

30. Farrington, D. P., Loeber, R., Elliot, D. S., Hawkins, D. J., Handel, D. B., Accord, J., Rowe, D., & Tremblay, R. (1990). Advancing knowledge about the onset of delinquency and crime. In B. Lahey & A. Kazdin (Eds.), *Advances in clinical child psychology* (vol. 13, pp. 283–342). New York: Plenum Press.

31. Biederman, J., Newcron, J., & Sprich, S. (1991). Comorbidity of attention deficit hyperactivity disorder with conduct, depression, anxiety, and other disorders. *American Journal of Psychiatry, 148,* 564–577.

32. Farrington, D. P., Loeber, R., & van Kammen, W. B. (1989). Long-term criminal outcomes of hyperactivity-impulsivity-attention deficit and conduct problems in childhood. In L. N. Robins & M. R. Rutter (Eds.), *Straight and devious pathways to adulthood* (pp. 62–81). New York: Cambridge University Press.

33. Barnes, M. T., Hudson, S. M., & Roberts, J. M. (2000). Characteristics of criminal defendants referred for psychiatric evaluation. *New Zealand Journal of Psychology, 29(2),* 61–65.

34. Frick, P. J., Lahey, B. B., Christ, M. A., Loeber, R., & Green, S. (1991). History of childhood behavior problems in biological relatives of boys with attention-deficit hyperactivity disorder and conduct disorder. *Journal of Clinical Child Psychology, 20(4),* 445–451.

35. Mednick, S. A., Gabrielli, W. F., & Hutchings, B. (1984). Genetic influences in criminal convictions: Evidence from an adoption court. *Science, 224,* 891–893.

36. Brown, G. L., & Goodwin, F. K. (1986). Human aggression: A biological perspective. In W. H. Reid, J. Dorr, D. Walker, & J. W. Bonner (Eds.), *Unmasking the psychopath: antisocial personality and related syndromes.* New York: Norton.

37. Coccaro, E. F., Siever, L. J., Klar, H. M., Maurer, G., Cochrane, K., Cooper, T. B., Mohs, R. C., & Davis, K. L. (1989). Serotonergic studies in patients with affective and personality disorders: Correlates with suicidal and impulsive aggressive behavior. *Archives of General Psychiatry, 46,* 587–599.

38. Ellis, L. (1991). Monamine oxidase and criminality: Identifying an apparent marker for antisocial behavior. *Journal of Research in Crime and Delinquency, 28,* 227–251.

39. Patterson, G. (1982). *Coercive family process.* Eugene, OR: Castalia.

40. Bronfenbrenner, U. (1979). *The ecology of human development: Experiments by nature and design.* Cambridge, MA: Harvard Press.

41. Webster-Stratton, C. (1990). Stress: A potential disruptor of parent perceptions and family interactions. *Journal of Clinical Child Psychology, 19,* 302–312.

42. Abidin, R. R. (1983). *Parenting stress index: Manual.* Charlottesville, VA: Pediatric Psychology Press.

43. Stoneman, A., Brody, G. H., & Burke, M. (1989). Marital quality, depression, and inconsistent parenting: Relationship with observed mother-child conflict. *American Orthopsychiatric Association, 59(1),* 105–117.

44. Frick, P. J., Lahey, B. B., Hardagen, S., & Hynd, G. W. (1989). Conduct problems in boys: Relations to maternal personality, marital satisfaction, and socioeconomic status. *Journal of Clinical Child Psychology, 18(2),* 114–120.

45. Brown, S. F. (1984). Social class, child maltreatment, and delinquent behavior. *Criminology, 22*, 259–278.
46. Cox, A. D., Puckering, C., Pound, A., & Mills, M. (1987). The impact of maternal depression on young people. *Journal of Child Psychology and Psychiatry, 28*, 917–928.
47. Frick, P. J., Lahey, B. B., Loeber, R., Stouthamer-Loeber, M., Christ, M. A., & Hanson, K. (1992). Familial risk factors to oppositional defiant disorder and conduct disorder: Parent psychopathology and maternal parenting. *Journal of Consulting and Clinical Psychology, 60*, 49–55.
48. Vanyukov, M., Moss, H. B., & Pliail, J. A. (1993). Antisocial symptoms in preadolescent boys and their parents: Association with cortisol. *Psychiatry Research, 46*, 9–17.

Chapter 2

1. Skinner, B. F. (1953). *Science and human behavior*. New York: Macmillan.
2. Van Houten, R. (1983). Punishment: From the animal laboratory to the applied setting. In S. Axelrod & J. Apsche (Eds.), *The effects of punishment on human behavior* (pp. 13–44). New York: Academic Press.
3. Azrin, N. H., & Besalel, V. A. (1980). *How to use over-correction*. Lawrence, KS: H & H Enterprises.
4. Weiner, H. (1962). Some effects of response-cost on human operant behavior. *Journal of the Experimental Analysis of Behavior, 5*, 201–208.
5. Bostow, D. E., & Bailey, J. B. (1969). Modification of severe disruptive and aggressive behavior using brief timeout and reinforcement procedures. *Journal of Applied Behavior Analysis, 2*, 31–37.
6. Williams, C. D. (1959). The elimination of tantrum behavior by extinction procedures. *Journal of Abnormal and Social Psychology, 59*, 269.
7. Hall, R. V., & Hall, M. C. (1980). *How to use planned ignoring*. Austin, TX: Pro-Ed.
8. Premack, D. (1964). Reinforcement of drinking by running: Effect of fixed ratio and reinforcement time. *Journal of the Experimental Analysis of Behavior, 7*(1), 91–96.
9. Ayllon, T., & Azrin, N. H. (1986). *The token economy: A motivational system for therapy and rehabilitation*. New York: Appleton-Century-Crofts.
10. O'Leary, K. D., Becker, W. C., Evans, M. B., & Saudargas, R. A. (1969). A token reinforcement program in a public school: A replication and systematic analysis. *Journal of Applied Behavior Analysis, 2*, 3–13.

Chapter 3

1. Horner, R. H., Sugai, G., Todd, A. W., & Lewis-Palmer, T. (2000). Elements of behavior support plans: A technical brief. *Exceptionality, 8*(3), 205–215.
2. Schopler, E., Van Bourgondien, M. E., & Bristol, M. M. (1993). *Preschool issues in autism*. New York: Plenum Press.

3. Schopler, E. (1988). *Individualized assessment and treatment for autistic and developmentally disabled children*. Baltimore: University Park Press.

Chapter 5

1. Glasser, W. (1965). *Reality therapy, a new approach to psychiatry*. New York: Harper & Row.

Chapter 6

1. Individuals with Disabilities Act Authorization (1990). Public Law 101-476. 20 U.S.C. 1401.
2. Warr-Leeper, G., Wright, N. A., & Mack, A. (1994). Language disabilities of antisocial boys in residential treatment. *Behavioral Disorders, 19*(3), 159–169.
3. Funk, J. B., & Ruppert, E. S. (1994). Language disorders and behavioral problems in preschool children. *Journal of Developmental and Behavioral Pediatrics, 5*(6), 357–360.
4. Piaget, J., & Inhelder, B. (1969). *The psychology of the child*. New York: Basic Books.
5. Luria, A. R. (1981). *Language and cognition*. New York: John Wiley & Sons. (Original work published 1979, Moscow.)
6. Fox, J., & McEvoy, M. (1993). Assessing and enhancing generalization and social validity of social-skills interventions with children and adolescents. *Behavior Modification, 17*, 339–366.
7. Horner, R. H., Dunlap, G., & Koegel, R. L. (Eds.). (1988). *Generalization and maintenance: Life style changes in applied settings*. New York: Paul H. Brooks Publishing Company.
8. Coie, J. D., Lockman, J. E., Terry, R., & Hyman, C. (1992). Predicting early adolescent disorder from childhood aggression and peer rejection. *Journal of Consulting and Clinical Psychology, 60*, 783–792.
9. Elliot, S. N., Racine, C. N., & Busse, R. T. (1995). Best practices in preschool social skills training. In A. Thomas & J. Grimes (Eds.), *Best practices in school psychology III* (pp. 1009–1020). Washington, DC: National Association of School Psychologists.
10. Elliot, S. N. (1998). Acceptability of behavioral treatments in educational settings. In J. C. Witts, S. N. Elliot, & F. M. Gresham (Eds.), *Handbook of behavior therapy in education* (pp. 121–150). New York: Plenum.
11. Dodge, K. A., & Crick, N. R. (1990). Social information-processing bases of aggressive behavior in children. *Personality and Social Psychology Bulletin, 16*, 8–22.
12. Gresham, F. M. (1995). Best practices in social skills training. In A. Thomas & J. Grimes (Eds.), *Best practices in school psychology III* (pp. 1021–1030). Washington, DC: National Association of School Psychologists.
13. Wandless, R. L., & Prinz, R. J. (1982). Methodological issues in conceptualizing and treating childhood social isolation. *Psychological Bulletin, 92*, 39–55.

14. Strain, P. S., & Fox, J. (1981). Peers as behavioral change agents for withdrawn class-mates. In B. B. Lahey & A. E. Kazdin (Eds.), *Advances in clinical child psychology* (vol. 4, pp. 167–198). New York: Plenum.

15. Gresham, F. M. (1981). Assessment of children's social skills. *Journal of School Psychology, 19*, 120–134.

16. Lentz, F. E. (1988). Reductive procedures. In J. Witt, S. Elliot, & F. Gresham (Eds.), *Handbook of behavior therapy in education* (pp. 439–460). New York: Plenum.

17. Henggeler, S. (1989). *Delinquency in adolescence.* Beverly Hills, CA: Sage Press.

18. Berler, E. S., Gross, A. M., & Drabman, R. S. (1982). Social skills training with children: Proceed with caution. *Journal of Applied Behavior Analysis, 15*, 41–53.

19. Bullis, M., Walker, H., & Sprague, J. R. (2001). A promise unfulfilled: Social skills training with at-risk and antisocial children and youth. *Exceptionality, 9*(1&2), 67–90.

20. Beelman, A., Pfingsten, R., & Loesel, F. (1994). Effects of training social competence in children: A meta-analysis of recent evaluation studies. *Journal of Clinical Child Psychology, 23*(3), 260–271.

21. Forness, S., Kavale, K., Blum, I., & Lloyd, J. (1997). A mega analysis of meta analyses: What works in special education and related services? *Teaching Exceptional Children, 13*(1), 4–9.

22. Kazdin, A. E. (1986). *Treatment of antisocial behavior in children and adolescents.* Homewood, IL: Dorsey Press.

23. Hawkins, J. D., Catalano, R. F., Kosterman, R., Abbott, R., & Hill, K. G. (1999). Preventing adolescent health-risk behaviors by strengthening protection during childhood. *Archives of Pediatrics and Adolescent Medicine, 153*, 226–234.

24. Freedman, B. J., Rosenthal, L., Donahoe, C. P., Schlundt, D. G., & McFall, R. M. (1978). A social-behavioral analysis of skill deficits in delinquent and nondelinquent boys. *Journal of Consulting and Clinical Psychology, 49*, 959–967.

25. Bandura, A. (1986). *Social foundations of thought and action: A social cognitive theory.* Englewood Cliffs, NJ: Prentice Hall.

26. Lockman, J. E., Coie, J. D., Underwood, M. K., & Terry, R. (1993). Effectiveness of social relations intervention program for aggressive and nonaggressive, rejected children. *Journal of Consulting and Clinical Psychology, 61*, 1053–1058.

27. Bierman, K. L., Miller, C. L., & Staub, S. D. (1987). Improving the social behavior and peer acceptance of rejected boys: Effects of social skills training with instructions and prohibitions. *Journal of Consulting and Clinical Psychology, 55*, 194–200.

Chapter 7

1. Hanf, C. A. (1969). A two-stage program for modifying maternal controlling during mother-child (M-C) interaction. Paper presented at the meeting of the Western Psychological Association, Vancouver.

2. Kazdin, A. E. (1985). *Treatment of antisocial behavior in children and adolescents*. Homewood, IL: Dorsey Press.

3. Patterson, G. R., Reid, J. B., Jones, R. R., & Conger, R. E. (1975). *A social learning approach to family intervention: Vol 1. Families with aggressive children*. Eugene, OR: Castalia.

4. Patterson, G. R. (1980). Mothers: The unacknowledged victims. With commentary by Eleanor E. Maccoby; with reply by the author. *Monographs of the Society for Research in Child Development, 45* (5 Serial No. 186).

5. Forehand, R., & McMahon, R. J. (1981). *Helping the noncompliant child: A clinician's guide to parent training*. New York: Guilford Press.

6. Webster-Stratton, C. (1981, Summer). Videotape modeling: A method of parent education. *Journal of Clinical Child Psychology, 10*(2), 93–98.

7. Webster-Stratton, C., Kolpacoff, M., & Hollinsworth, T. (1988). Self-administered videotape therapy for families with conduct-problem children: Comparison of two cost-effective treatments and a control group. *Journal of Consulting and Clinical Psychology, 56*, 558–566.

8. Hall, P. S., & Braun. V. R. (1988, June). Punishment: A consumer's perspective. *TASH Newsletter*, p. 9.

9. Patterson, G. (1971). *Families: Applications of social learning to family life*. Champaign, IL: Research Press, pp. 25 & 26.

10. Brofenbrenner, U. (1979). *The ecology of human development: Experiments by nature and by design*. Cambridge, MA: Harvard University Press, p. 60.

11. Hall, P. S. (1992). Applied humanism: A model for normalized behavior programming. *Journal of Humanistic Education and Development, 31*, 22–32.

12. Dreikurs R., & Grey, L. (1968). *Logical consequences*. New York: Meredith Press.

13. Abidin, R. R. (1983). *Parenting stress index: Manual*. Charlottesville, VA: Pediatric Psychology Press.

14. Premack, D. (1959). Toward empirical behavior law: Positive reinforcement. *Psychological Review, 66*, 219–233.

15. Serketich, W. J., & Dumas, J. (1996). The effectiveness of behavior parent training to modify antisocial behavior in children: A meta-analysis. *Behavior Therapy, 27*, 171–186.

16. Bernal, M. E., Klinnert, M. D., & Schultz, L. A. (1980). Outcome evaluation of behavioral parent training and client-centered parent counseling for children with conduct problems. *Journal of Applied Behavioral Analysis, 13*, 677–691.

17. Kazdin, A. E. (1997). Parent management training: Evidence, outcomes, and issues. *Journal of the American Academy of Child and Adolescent Psychiatry, 31*(10), 1349–1356.

18. Breiner, J. L., & Forehand, R. (1981). An assessment of the effects of parent training on clinic-referred children's school behavior. *Behavior Assessment, 3*, 31–42.

19. Patterson, G. R. (1974). Retraining aggressive boys by their parents: Review of the literature and follow-up evaluation. In F. Lowry (Ed.), *Symposium on the seriously disturbed preschool child. Canadian Psychiatric Association Journal, 42*, 471–481.

20. Armbruster, P., & Kazdin, A. E. (1994). Attrition in child psychotherapy. In T. H. Ollendick & R. J. Prinz (Eds.), *Advances in clinical child psychology* (vol. 16, pp. 81–108). New York: Plenum.
21. Diamond, G., Bernal, G., & Flores-Ortiz, Y. (1991). Engagement and recruitment for family therapy research in community settings. *Contemporary Family Therapy, 13,* 255–274.
22. Miller, W. R. (1985). Motivation for treatment: A review with special emphasis on alcoholism. *Psychological Bulletin, 98,* 846–851.
23. Wahler, R. G. (1980). The insular mother: Her problems in parent-child treatment. *Journal of Applied Behavior Analysis, 13,* 207–219.
24. Eyberg, S. M., Boggs, S. R., & Rodriquez, C. M. (1992). Relationships between maternal parenting stress and child disruptive behavior. *Child and Family Behavior Therapy, 14,* 1–10.
25. Forehand, R. L., Furey, W. M., & McMahon, R. J. (1984). The role of maternal distress in parenting training program to modify child noncompliance. *Behavioral Psychotherapy, 12,* 93–108.
26. Webster-Stratton, C., & Hammond, M. (1990). Predictors of treatment outcome in parent training for families with conduct problem children. *Behavior Therapy, 21,* 319–337.
27. Dumas, J. E. (1984). Child, adult-interactional, and socioeconomic settings events as predictors of parent training outcome. *Education and Treatment of Children, 7,* 351–364.
28. Kazdin, A. E., Esveldt-Dawson, K., French, N. H., & Unis, A. S. (1987). Effects of parent management training and problem-solving skills training combined in the treatment of antisocial child behavior. *Journal of the American Academy of Child and Adolescent Psychiatry, 36,* 416–424.
29. Ducharme, J. M., Popynick, M., Pontes, E., & Steele, S. (1996). Errorless compliance to parental requests III: Group parent training with parent observational data and long-term follow-up. *Behavior Therapy, 27,* 363–372.

Chapter 8

1. Reitsma-Street, M., Offord, D. R., & Finch, T. (1985). Pairs of same-sexed siblings discordant for antisocial behavior. *British Journal of Psychiatry, 146,* 415–423.
2. Reis, D. S. (1975). *Central neurotransmitters in aggressive behaviors: Neural basis of violence and aggression.* St. Louis, MO: Green.
3. Campbell, M., Small, A., Green, W. H., Jennings, S. J., Perry, R., Bennett, W. G., & Anderson, L. (1984). Behavior efficacy of haloperidol and lithium carbonate: A comparison in hospitalized aggressive children with conduct disorder. *Archives of General Psychiatry, 41,* 650–656.

4. Cowdry, R. W., & Gardner, D. L. (1988). Pharmacotherapy of borderline personality disorder: Alprazolam, carbamazepine, trifluoperazine, and tranylcypromine. *Archives of General Psychiatry, 45*, 111–119.

5. Ghaziuddin, N., & Alessi, N. E. (1992). An open clinical trial of trazodone in aggressive children. *Journal of Child and Adolescent Psychopharmacology, 2*, 291–297.

6. Kafantaris, V., Campbell, M., Padron-Gayol, M. V., Small, A. M., Locasio, J. J., & Rosenberg, C. R. (1992). Carbamazepine in hospitalized aggressive conduct-disordered children: An open pilot study. *Psychopharmacological Bulletin, 28*, 719–723.

7. McDaniel, K. D. (1986). Pharmacological treatment of psychiatric and neurodevelopmental disorders in children and adolescents (part 1). *Clinical Pediatrics, 25*, 65–71.

8. Kranzler, H. R. (1988). Use of buspirone in an adolescent with overanxious disorder. *Journal of the American Academy of Child and Adolescent Psychiatry, 27*, 789–790.

9. Zametkin, A. J., Nordahl, T. E., Gross, M., King, C., Semple, W. E., & Rumsey, J. (1990). Cerebral glucose metabolism in adults with hyperactivity of childhood onset. *New England Journal of Medicine, 323*, 1361–1366.

10. Lura, A. R. (1973). *The working brain*. London: Penguin Books.

11. Greenhill, L. L. (2001). Clinical effects of stimulant medication in ADHD. In M. V. Solanto, A. F. T. Arnsten, & F. X. Castellanos (Eds.), *Stimulant drugs and ADHD: Basic and clinical neuroscience* (pp. 737–745). New York: Oxford University Press.

12. Conners, K. C. (1997). Conners' Rating Scale Revised-Short Form: Technical manual. North Tonawanda, NY: Multi-Health Systems.

13. Greenberg, L. (1988). Tests of Variables of Attention. Los Alamidos, CA: Universal Attention Disorders.

14. Conners, K. C. (1990). Conners' Continuous Performance Test. North Tonawanda, NY: Multi-Health Systems.

15. Richters, J. E., Arnold, L. E., Jensen, P. J., Abikoff, H., Conners, C. K., Greenhill, L. L., Hechtman, L., Hinshaw, S. P., Pelham, W. E., & Swanson, J. M. (1995). NIMH collaborative multi-site, multi-modal treatment study of children with ADHD: I. Background and rationale. *Journal of the American Academy of Child and Adolescent Psychiatry, 34*, 987–1000.

16. Anastopoulus, A. D., & Shelton, T. L. (2001). *Assessing attention-deficit/hyperactivity disorder*. New York: Kluwer.

17. Beelmann, A., Pfingsten, U., & Losel, F. (1994). Effects of training social competence in children: A meta-analysis of recent evaluation studies. *Journal of Clinical Child Psychology, 23*, 260–271.

18. Forman, S. G. (1980). A comparison of cognitive training and response cost procedures in modifying aggressive behavior of elementary school children. *Behavior Therapy, 11*, 594–600.

19. Lockman, J. E., Nelson, W. M. III, & Sims, J. P. (1981). A cognitive behavior program for use with aggressive children. *Journal of Clinical Child Psychology, 10*, 146–148.

20. Lockman, J. E., Burch, P. R., Curry, J. F., & Lampron, L. B. (1984). Treatment and generalization effects of cognitive-behavioral and goal-setting interventions with aggressive boys. *Journal of Consulting and Clinical Psychology, 52,* 915–916.

21. Kendall, P. C., Reber, M., McLeer, S., Epps, J., & Ronan, K. R. (1990). Cognitive-behavior treatment of conduct-disordered children. *Cognitive Therapy and Research, 14,* 279–297.

22. Kendall, P. C., & Braswell, L. (1985). *Cognitive-behavior therapy for impulsive children.* New York: Guilford Press.

23. Kazdin, A. E., Esveldt-Dawson, K., French, N. H., & Unis, A. S. (1987). Problem-solving skills training and relationship therapy in the treatment of antisocial child behavior. *Journal of Consulting and Clinical Psychology, 55,* 76–85.

24. Webster-Stratton, C., & Hammond, M. (1997). Treating children with early-onset conduct problems: A comparison of child and parent training interventions. *Journal of Consulting and Clinical Psychology, 65,* 93–109.

25. Webster-Stratton, C. (1991). *Dinosaur social skills and problem-solving training manual.* Unpublished manuscript.

26. McGee, J. J., Menolascino, F. J., Hobbs, D. C., & Menousek, P. E. (1987). *Gentle teaching: A nonaversive approach to helping persons with mental retardation.* New York: Human Sciences Press.

27. Schopler, E. (1978). Individualized assessment and treatment for autistic and developmentally disabled children. Baltimore: University Park Press.

28. Forehand, R., Furey, W., & McMahon, R. (1984). The role of maternal distress in a parent training program to modify child noncompliance. *Behavioral Psychotherapy, 12,* 93–108.

29. Patterson, G. R., & Forgatch, M. S. (1995). Predicting future clinical adjustment from treatment outcome and process variables. *Psychological Assessment, 7(3),* 275–285.

30. Webster-Stratton, C., Hollinsworth, T., & Kolpacoff, M. (1989). The long-term effectiveness and clinical significance of three cost-effective training programs for families with conduct-problem children. *Journal of Consulting and Clinical Psychology, 57(4),* 550–553.

31. Loeber, R. (1991). Antisocial behavior more enduring than changeable? *Journal of the American Academy of Child and Adolescent Psychiatry, 30,* 393–397.

32. Hall, P. S., & Wick, B. C. (1991). The relationship between ocular functions and reading achievement. *Journal of Pediatric Ophthalmology & Strabismus, 28(1),* 17–19.

Chapter 9

1. McGee, J. J., Menolascino, F. J., Hobbs, D. C., & Menousek, P. E. (1987). *Gentle teaching: A nonaversive approach for helping persons with mental retardation.* New York: Human Sciences Press.

2. Hall, P. S. (1992). Applied humanism: A model for normalized behavior programming. *Journal of Humanistic Education and Development, 31*, 22–32.

3. Dreikurs, R., & Soltz, V. (1964). *Children: The challenge.* New York: Duell, Sloan, & Pearce.

4. Ahlstrom, W. M., & Havighurst, R. J. (1971). *400 Losers.* San Francisco: Jossey-Bass, Inc.

5. Perske, R. (1972). The dignity of risk and the mentally retarded. *Mental Retardation, 10*(1), 24–26.

6. Hall, P. S. (1989, September). Teaching for behavior change. *Counterpoint,* p. 3.

7. Hall, P. S., & Braun, V. R. (1988, June). Punishment: A consumer's perspective. *TASH Newsletter,* p. 3.

8. Dreikurs, R., & Grey, L. (1968). *Logical consequences.* New York: Meredith Press.

9. Hall, P. S., & Hall, N. D. (2002). Hiring and retaining direct-care staff: After fifty years of research, what do we know? *Mental Retardation, 40*(3), 201–211.

10. Hall, P. S. (1992). Applied humanism: A model for normalized behavior programming. *Journal of Humanistic Educational Development, 31*, 22–32.

Index

Note:
Information in figures is indicated by an italic *f*.
Information in samples or case studies is indicated by an italic *s*.

About the Authors

PHILIP S. HALL is a psychologist with 30 years of experience working with children who have challenging behaviors. For the past 10 years, he was Director of the School Psychology Program at Minot State University in Minot, North Dakota. During that time, Hall provided a comprehensive clinic for children with oppositional and defiant behaviors and their families. Recently retired from academic work, he continues to consult widely to schools faced with students who have challenging behavior or learning problems.

NANCY D. HALL has worked for the past 25 years in educational administration. Fifteen of those years were as an elementary school principal, where she worked closely with special needs children, their parents, teachers, and community service providers. She is currently Vice President of Academic Affairs at Minot State University.

Related ASCD Resources: Educating Oppositional and Defiant Children

At the time of publication, the following ASCD resources were available; for the most up-to-date information about ASCD resources, go to www.ascd.org. ASCD stock numbers are noted in parentheses.

Audiotapes

Conscious Classroom Management: Bringing Out the Best in Students and Teachers by Rick Smith (#202248)

Creating a Caring Classroom: Activities That Promote Intellectual, Ethical, and Emotional Growth by Ward Downs and Jan Utterback (#299186)

Effective Discipline: Getting Beyond Rewards and Punishment by Marvin Marshall (#297190)

Redirecting Student Refusal and Resistance Toward Respectful and Responsible Behavior by Louise Griffith and Pat Voss (#201095)

Transforming Hostile Behaviors in the Classroom by Robert Hanson (#297184)

Win Win Discipline by Patricia Kyle (#202258)

Networks

Visit the ASCD Web site (www.ascd.org) and search for "networks" for information about professional educators who have formed groups around topics like "Instructional Supervision." Look in the "Network Directory" for current facilitators' addresses and phone numbers.

Online Resources

Visit ASCD's Web site (ascd.org) for the following professional development opportunities.

Educational Leadership: Understanding Learning Differences (entire issue, November 2001) Excerpted articles online free; entire issue online and accessible to ASCD members (Go to www.ascd.org, click on "Publica-

tions," and go to the *Educational Leadership* page.)

Professional Development Online: *Classroom Management: Building Relationships for Better Learning*, among others (Go to www.ascd.org and click on "Professional Development.") (for a small fee; password protected)

Print Products

ADD/ADHD Alternatives in the Classroom by Thomas Armstrong (#199273)

Discipline with Dignity by Richard L. Curwin and Allen N. Mendler (#199235)

Power Struggles: Successful Techniques for Educators by Allen N. Mendler (#301233)

Teaching Conflict Resolution with the Rainbow Kids Program by Barbara Porro (#101247)

Videotapes

Catch Them Being Good (3 videos with facilitator's guide) (#614162)

Managing Today's Classroom (3 videos with facilitator's guide) (#498027)

Teaching Students with Learning Disabilities in the Regular Classroom (2 videos with a facilitator's guide) (#402084)

For more information, visit us on the World Wide Web (http://www.ascd.org), send an e-mail message to member@ascd.org, call the ASCD Service Center (1-800-933-ASCD or 703-578-9600, then press 2), send a fax to 703-575-5400, or write to Information Services, ASCD, 1703 N. Beauregard St., Alexandria, VA 22311-1714 USA.